Self Storage
and
The Occupant

Plays by
William Damkoehler

Fomite
Burlington, VT

ISBN-13: 978-1-953236-90-6
Library of Congress Control Number: 2023931546
Fomite
58 Peru Street
Burlington, VT 05401
03-10-2023

For Cym — my muse, critic, humor savant, and exuberant co-conspirator in art and life…

Praise for William Damkoehler's Writing

"William Damkoehler's witty, and oft times ferociously funny, duet—SELF STORAGE and THE OCCUPANT—reveals to the discerning eye a seasoned dramatist's attention to detail and a strict focus for converting a native ear, evolved and trained, to veritably 'talk the talk' in these two flawless bodies of work — both contemporary gems of genuine human dialogue…"
—Fred Rosenblum, bawdy American poet whose latest collection is entitled *Tramping Solo*.

"William Damkoehler miraculously uncovers worlds of complexity in the unlikely setting of a humble storage unit. With nods to Beckett, Shakespeare, Chaplin and Groucho Marx, he manages to infuse his eminently actable dialogue with a playfulness that poses deep existential questions. As his characters struggle with issues of life, death, loss and bewilderment, they find wonder and relief in moments of transcendence that echo centuries of theatrical magic. As a playwright Damkoehler understands that every one of us keeps a protected self under lock and key; and as a life-long theatre artist he understands that it is often through the power of art, magic, and imagination that we are able, for a moment at least, to raise the metal door that protects our fragile inner lives. SELF STORAGE is a miracle of artful simplicity – I can't imagine a mature actor who wouldn't be thrilled to play any one of these roles."
—Brian McEleney, professional actor, director, playwright, Founding Director, Brown University/Trinity Rep M.F.A. Acting Program

"With humor, mystery, and a touch of pathos, SELF STORAGE is a trim, ninety minute play featuring four wonderfully rich roles for veteran actors. Easy to produce, and a pleasure to perform, it spins a funny, rich story from one of the most quotidian-yet-tantalizing riddles in

modern society — what the heck is in that guy's storage container?"
—Tyler Dobrowski, producer and theater director.

"Within these two plays, we find deeply flawed characters hell-bent on creating situations that are both hilarious and heartwarming. Through their underlying stories, we dip our toes into vital drama which feels timely and important to our current culture. Bravo to Bill Damkoehler for sharing this thoroughly entertaining work with us."
—Kate Porter, author, *Lessons In Disguise* (Konstellation Press, 2017]

"I just love SELF STORAGE! Bill's play is theatrical, smart, funny — and trust me — you don't know where it's going."
—Phyllis Kay, professional actor

"I have loved Bill Damkoehler as an actor, director, and human being for forty years, and now know him as a really special playwright. SELF STORAGE — his four-character play in which I played a role in the first workshop version — is simply remarkable: surprising, magical, and indelibly human. This play has everything for a wonderful night of theater. Bill is a great man of the theater and I applaud him once again!"
—Fred Sullivan, Jr., professional actor, director, theater educator.

Contents

Introduction

After forty years of steady work as an Equity professional actor in Trinity Repertory Company's (Providence, Rhode Island) resident acting company — a dream job for an American actor — I finally hung up the old Sock and Buskin; forty years of six-days-and-eight-shows-per-week can take a toll. The Equity pension I earned, plus Social Security, allows me now to focus on my writing, and my actor's sensibility compels me to write plays with characters complex and challenging — characters actors would love to tangle with. SELF STORAGE and THE OCCUPANT are two such plays.

Both plays have been considered for full production by major regional theaters — a labor that can eat up years between time of commitment to opening night; and I don't know how many productive years I have left to me. Besides, the arrival of the Covid pandemic precluded all theater production worldwide. These plays did receive, however, staged readings, or "Readers Theater" treatments, and were very warmly received. So it is with this in mind that I offer SELF STORAGE and THE OCCUPANT in this Fomite volume. The texts of these plays contain stage directions that are meant to not only guide a full staging, but also to be read aloud and provide context and forward momentum in a Readers Theater environment. Actors can fully perform from memory or from open scripts, as desired. Fully-staged productions of SELF STORAGE and THE OCCUPANT will employ stage tricks and "magic." After all, it's Theater. For questions about producing, or about any other aspect of these plays, please contact me through my website: www.billdam.com

And for those who enjoy reading plays in order to fully produce them if only in the Theater Of The Mind, your curtain rises when you turn this page…

SELF STORAGE

"Man Throws 3-Year-Old Son, Self From Manhattan Rooftop"
— *LA Times*, December 23, 2013

Original Cast, Trinity Workshop
Trinity Repertory Company
Providence, RI
October, 2014

JERRY..................Fred Sullivan, Jr.
PETRA..................Phyllis Kay
MARCUS..............Brian McEleney
THE LODGER..........George Spelvin

SELF STORAGE

Cast of Characters

JERRY: Male. Early sixties. He's lived a hard life. Guilt-ridden. And it shows.

PETRA: Female. Mid-fifties. Professional. Wears makeup, does her hair. To her, the world is a fingernail scratching a blackboard.

MARCUS: Late sixties. Innocent. Childlike.

THE LODGER: Indeterminate gender. Indeterminate age. Does not speak.

Scene: A self storage facility in an American city.
Time: The Present. Summer. Late afternoon.

> *A self storage facility built of concrete blocks. The three units visible on stage, numbered 247, 248, and 249, are fronted by large rolling metal garage-type doors which can open to reveal 10' x 10' storage spaces. The doors are freshly painted a deep red. Over each of the doors is a shaded light fixture. Above the whole structure is a sign reading: "SELF STORAGE — FIRST MONTH FREE."*
> *As the scene begins, the door to the stage right space, number 247, is open, the other two — 248 and 249 — are closed. The open space, number 247, is cluttered with odd pieces of furniture, cardboard boxes, and plastic storage bins — many of which are labeled with the names of two women: "Rosalind" and "Kate." On the ground downstage of 247 are two such plastic bins, both labeled "Rosalind," and an old chair. Eventually a man, JERRY, emerges from the space. HE is lugging a plastic storage bin — this one labeled "Kate" — which he places on the tarmac next to the bins labeled "Rosalind." JERRY pulls off the lid of one "Rosalind" bin and lays it aside. HE drags the old chair in*

*front of the bin, sits down, peers into the bin. HE reaches
into it and pushes a few items around, none of which we
are able to see. HE pulls his hand back, stares into the bin,
shakes his head slowly. A woman, PETRA, enters from
stage left. JERRY turns his head and watches her as SHE
unlocks the padlock on the stage left storage space and
removes the lock. There is a sliding latch SHE must open.
SHE struggles with it. JERRY watches PETRA struggle for
a moment, then:*

JERRY

You're doing it wrong.

PETRA stiffens, looks toward JERRY.

PETRA

Are you talking to me?

JERRY

Yeah. You're not doing it right. Want me to help you?

PETRA

I'll do it myself, thank you very much.

JERRY

Okay, but I know the trick to it. If you step down on the handle it
takes the strain off the latch, see? Then you can slide—

PETRA

I know that.

JERRY

Oops… Sorry.

PETRA

I just keep forgetting to do it.

JERRY

Sorry. I thought you were new. I've never seen—

PETRA

I'm not new. I know how this works. Thank you very much.

JERRY

No problem…

*PETRA steps down with some vehemence on the handle,
slides the latch, and rolls up the steel door of unit number
249, revealing a storage space as cluttered as JERRY's.*

JERRY (cont'd)

There you go.

PETRA

Mm hmm…

*PETRA enters the space and disappears among the clutter.
JERRY makes an obscene gesture toward her vanishing figure.
HE sits down again and peers into the open "Rosalind" bin on
the ground. HE slowly shakes his head. PETRA appears and
disappears, looking in bins, opening boxes, etcetera. JERRY
speaks to PETRA as she comes and goes:*

JERRY
(Speaks loudly, so PETRA will be sure to hear him.)

Sorry. Got off on the wrong foot there, I guess… Haven't seen you
here before, so… Sorry… Whew! All this stuff! Kinda shocks me
every time I open my unit and see it all, you know? Really shouldn't
have kept it all this time. What a burden, huh? Expensive, too, with
the rent here going up and up. But I can't get rid of it, you know? It
would seem a violation of… I don't know what. I mean, it's useless to
me now. I've moved on, you know…? I don't know…

*PETRA remains hidden somewhere in her unit. JERRY
goes silent, replaces the lid on the bin. HE slides the chair
over and opens the bin labeled "Kate." From the bin HE
lifts out a sturdy, plain, cardboard box about the size of a
birthday cake. The box is tied with string. HE sets this box
on the ground and again reaches into the bin. HE pulls out
a gun: a grim-looking .38 revolver. HE stands up, turns the
gun over and over in HIS hands, when another person,
THE LODGER, enters from stage right. THE LODGER
is dressed in a high-collared shirt that obscures the face, a*

flowing cape, and a theatrical broad-brimmed, feathered
hat which sits on a head of long dark hair. JERRY quickly
hides the gun behind his back. THE LODGER crosses in
front of JERRY, who reflexively greets THE LODGER.

JERRY

Good afternoon…

THE LODGER stops, turns to JERRY and, with many
ruffles and flourishes, executes a deep, theatrical bow,
sweeping the ground with the hat, then wordlessly
approaches the center door, number 248, appears to unlock
it, steps down on the handle to relieve the strain on the
sliding latch, slides it, rolls the door part way up, ducks
under it and rolls the door back down from the inside.
JERRY quickly puts the revolver back in the bin, stares at the
door behind which THE LODGER has disappeared. After a
moment, HE crosses to PETRA's space and calls to her:

JERRY (cont'd)

Hello? Hello? Hello!

PETRA

What?

PETRA emerges from her space. JERRY points a finger at
the center door, speaks in a stage whisper:

JERRY

Did you see that?

PETRA

What?

JERRY

Somebody just went in there. Somebody just opened up two-forty-
eight and went in.

PETRA

So?

JERRY

I mean, he went inside and closed the door. He's still inside.

PETRA looks at the closed door of 248.

PETRA

It's locked.

JERRY looks at the door. It does, indeed, appear to have its lock in place.

JERRY

That's… You're right. It's… It's locked. And it's a standard vacancy lock, not a renter's lock.

PETRA

And it's against the rules to close the door when you're inside. They don't allow it. Read your contract. It's against the rules.

JERRY

I know. But…

JERRY eases over to 248 and carefully puts his ear against the door.

PETRA

They don't want live-ins. It's against the rules to inhabit a space. If you close the door while you're inside a space, you're inhabiting. They call it inhabiting. No live-ins. They don't allow it. No living being, plant or animal, is allowed. Haven't you read your contract?

JERRY

Of course I've read it. Not every single word, but…

(Still listening at the door:)

Nothing…

JERRY takes his ear from the door and reaches for the lock on 248.

PETRA

No tampering with the locks—

JERRY quickly pulls his hand away.

                          JERRY
I know, I know. Weird… He passed right by me, dressed real strange
— with a black cape and a big black hat, with a feather! I said "Hi," or
something, he took a bow, then he—

                          PETRA
He took a what?

                          JERRY
A bow.

                          PETRA
From your unit?

                          JERRY
From my…?

                          PETRA
Unit? He took something from your unit?

                          JERRY
No. Oh. No. He took a bow. A "bow." Like this:

          He demonstrates as best HE can THE LODGER's
          theatrical bow.

                          PETRA
Oh. A "bow." I thought he took something from your unit.

                          JERRY
No. He bowed to me, then he unlocked the door, went in, and rolled
the door back down.

                          PETRA
That's against the rules.

                          JERRY
I know that. Don't keep— I'm just saying, regulations or no, there's
someone in there.

PETRA

They don't want live-ins. And they don't want… other things you can
do in there. With the door closed.

JERRY

Yeah, well, there's some that follow the rules and some that don't.
People are different.

PETRA

No, they're not. People are all the same. Everywhere.

JERRY

Right. Right. We're all human. Right?

PETRA

"Human?" "Human?" Don't make me laugh…

> PETRA turns, retreats into the jumble of 249. JERRY
> sticks his tongue out at PETRA behind her back, flips
> her the bird, then walks past the closed door of 248 to
> his own space and his open bin on the ground — the one
> labeled "Kate." HE sits down in the chair and peers into
> the bin. Then HE looks over his shoulder at 248, stands,
> and walks carefully to the closed door. HE looks it over,
> up and down, then reaches his hand out toward the lock,
> but pulls it back abruptly just before making contact with
> it, glancing reflexively at where HE last saw PETRA. HE
> scowls, backs away from 248, turns to the bin labeled
> "Rosalind" he had been examining, hefts it from the
> ground, and lugs it back into his unit, leaving behind
> the "Kate" bin and the other "Rosalind" bin. Just as HE
> disappears among the junk, a golf cart rolls on, very
> slowly, from stage left. It makes a loud electric whine as it
> travels at a snail's pace toward stage right. MARCUS —
> a white-haired gentleman dressed in khaki work clothes
> — is driving it. HE leans eagerly forward, concentrating
> on the road ahead. Eventually, MARCUS and the cart
> disappear stage right just as JERRY emerges from among
> his stuff. HE has apparently heard MARCUS pass by. HE
> calls toward stage right:

JERRY

Marcus? Marcus?

MARCUS
(From offstage.)

Yes?

The sound of the golf cart motor stops. There is a brief silence. Then the electric whine starts again, accompanied by a "beep-beep-beep" warning. The cart appears, backing in from stage right. MARCUS, clumsy with the cart's controls, makes a few, jerky, false stops-and-starts till HE finally brings the cart to rest center stage, in front of the door of 248.

JERRY

Ah. Good afternoon.

MARCUS

Good afternoon.

JERRY

Visiting your books?

MARCUS

No. No. I am working today. I am working.

JERRY

Ah. Well. No rest for the wicked.

MARCUS

Meaning me?

JERRY

What?

MARCUS

Meaning me? I'm wicked?

JERRY

No. I— No. It's just a… I mean, I am sorry you have to work. But, then, it's good you have a job, hmm?

MARCUS

I would rather spend time with my books. Did I tell you I have filled two units here already with my books?

JERRY

Two? No. Two?

MARCUS

Two. And I may need to rent a third, if I acquire even a dozen more. So many books. And I've recently developed an interest in Graphic Novels. Picture Books! I opened up some room in my first unit when I sold my comic book collection, but now I'm filling that up with these wonderful Picture Books. And my comic book money is all but exhausted. I have had to take on this job to continue to pay the rent on the units I need to store all my books. But now I have no time to even visit my books, let alone read them.

JERRY

Yes. Marcus... Do you know... Are there vacancies here? Are there any vacancies? Here?

MARCUS

Vacancies? Yes. One.

JERRY

One?

MARCUS

One vacancy.

JERRY

So, you are not full?

MARCUS

There is one vacancy.

JERRY

One. You're sure?

MARCUS

One.

JERRY

I had the impression you were full.

MARCUS

No. No. There is one vacancy.

JERRY

One.

MARCUS

One.

JERRY

And, which—?

MARCUS

This one.

MARCUS jerks his thumb toward the closed door of 248.

JERRY

It's not rented, then?

MARCUS

Look at the lock. That's how you can tell if a unit is vacant. That is one of our standard vacancy locks. We have the master key. It's not a renter's personal lock. That's a standard vacancy lock.

JERRY

So it really is a vacancy?

MARCUS

Yes. Because that is a standard vacancy lock. It is also the unit I may need myself, if I add to my book collection.

JERRY

Well, what would you say if I told you I just saw someone go in there and shut the door?

MARCUS

I would say: "That's against the rules."

JERRY

Aha. But all the same, someone is in there. Someone unlocked the standard vacancy lock, opened the door, went inside and closed the door.

MARCUS

But it's locked.

JERRY

So it appears. So it appears. I didn't check it because it's against the rules to tamper, right? And I follow the rules... these days. But you could check. It's a security breach, isn't it? I mean, you've got to be extra careful these days, right?

MARCUS

I could. I could check.

JERRY

You should. You should check.

MARCUS

That's part of my job. Checking spaces.

JERRY

Do you have the master key?

MARCUS

Yes.

JERRY

Open it, then, and see for yourself.

(Hurries over to the open door of 249 and calls into the jumble of PETRA's space:)

Hello? Hello? Come out and see this!

MARCUS

But it's at the office.

JERRY

What?

MARCUS

The key. The master key is at the office.

JERRY

Can you get it?

MARCUS

Well, of course I can. The Boss has given me access to the master key.

JERRY

Then get it. There's something really suspicious going on in there, I tell you.

MARCUS

Oh, boy! This is exciting! I'll get the key and I'll check the space!

(HE looks over his shoulder and starts up the golf cart, but it goes forward instead of in reverse. HE stops the cart.)

Part of my job. Checking spaces.

MARCUS again looks over his shoulder and starts up the cart again. This time it goes in reverse, "beep-beeping" as it and MARCUS disappear stage left. JERRY calls again into the open space of 249, PETRA's unit:

JERRY

Hello? Hello?!

(HE approaches the jumble of stuff in 249.)

Helloooo?!

PETRA
(Calling from deep within her space.)

What do you want?!

JERRY again speaks to PETRA in an exaggerated stage whisper...

JERRY

Marcus is going to open the door! Come out and see this!

PETRA
(from within)

I can't. I'm looking for something…

JERRY

You won't want to miss this!

Suddenly PETRA screams.

PETRA
(from within)

OH MY GOD!

JERRY

What? Miss?! What's the matter? MISS?!

*PETRA emerges from her unit. SHE is holding a wrinkled
sheet of newspaper.*

JERRY (cont'd)

What happened? Are you alright?

PETRA waves the page of newspaper toward JERRY.

PETRA

Horrible. Oh my god, how can people be so horrible…?

JERRY

What do you mean?

PETRA

I was unwrapping something… and I read… this…

*PETRA, indicating a certain headline, hands the sheet of
paper to JERRY, who scans the paper for a few seconds,
then:*

JERRY

Oh. You mean—

PETRA

A fifty-two-story apartment building…

JERRY
(*Reads from the paper:*) "Man Throws Three-Year-Old Son, Self, From Roof"

There is a slight pause.

PETRA
I'll never understand.

JERRY
Mm.

PETRA
Horrible. A little child.

JERRY
Awful. Yes. Some people...

JERRY hands the crumpled sheet back to PETRA, who glances at it, then shouts:

PETRA
GOOD CHRIST!

JERRY
What?

PETRA, indicating another headline, hands the paper back to JERRY. HE reads:

JERRY(cont'd)
"Alleged Beating Leaves Two-Year-Old Boy Brain-Dead"

PETRA
Horrible! People are so... horrible! A two-year-old boy!

JERRY
Horrible. That's for sure.

JERRY hands the crumpled sheet back to PETRA, who glances at it, then shouts:

PETRA

JEEZUS GOD!

JERRY

No!

> *PETRA, indicating another headline, hands the paper*
> *back to JERRY.*

JERRY (cont'd)

You mean: *(Reads:)* "Man Stabs Ex-Wife, Daughter, To Death, Slits Own Wrists"? or did you mean: *(Reads:)* "Newborn Girl Found Beaten And Burned In A Trashcan"?

PETRA
(Shouts in reaction.)

HOLY MOTHER OF GOD! A *newborn*?! In a *trashcan*?!

JERRY

Oh. Sorry. I thought you saw that one. I'm sorry.

> *JERRY hands the crumpled sheet back to PETRA, who*
> *glances at it, again shouts:*

PETRA

HOLY MOTHERFUCKING SHIT!

JERRY

Oh, no…

> *PETRA, indicating another headline, hands the paper*
> *back to JERRY.*

JERRY (cont'd)

(Reads:) "Twelve-Year-Old Boy Shoots Homeless Man In Head, Leaves Him To Die"

PETRA
(On the verge of tears.)

Is there no kindness anywhere? No mercy?

JERRY

You would hope so, wouldn't you?

PETRA
(Weeps openly.)

I'm sorry! I never use vulgar language! But people are such animals! Savage, horrible, loathsome scum! I hate every single person who walks the face of this godforsaken earth!

JERRY, examines the paper, then:

JERRY

NO! NO-O-O-O-O!

PETRA

Oh, God, now what?

JERRY
(Reads:) "Democrats Set To Sweep Elections"!
(HE smiles broadly at his joke.)

PETRA

Demo—?

(Slight pause.)
That's not funny!

JERRY

Sorry. I'm just trying to lighten—

PETRA

To deliberately go up fifty-two stories... step by step... and throw a child off a roof... a little child...his own son! *(She weeps.)* Unforgivable.

JERRY

Well, he paid the price...

PETRA

Who?

JERRY

The father.

PETRA

How did he pay?

JERRY

He's dead. Threw himself off, too.

PETRA

Did he, though? Did he pay?

JERRY

He's dead!

PETRA

Dead or not, I can't forgive him.

JERRY

I doubt he much cares.

PETRA

And suicide? What's less forgivable than suicide?

JERRY

I get it, though… *(Reading from the newspaper:)* "Man Throws Three-Year-Old Son, Self, From Roof"… The instant the kid leaves his hands, the horror of what he just did hits him. No matter how psycho he is, it hits him. So he pretty much would have to throw himself off, too. He'd have to. I get that. Same with the guy who slit his own wrists. I get that. I know I would. Stab my ex and my kid? I'd slit my wrists, too. The guilt…

PETRA snatches the paper away from JERRY.

PETRA

What kind of person are you anyway? Sick? Like everyone else?

JERRY

No, I— I'm just saying I get it. You know. You snap. It happens. Go crazy. Lose your temper. Whatever. Really hurt somebody. Kill them… You throw the kid over? You jump. Period. Pay the price. Eye-for-an-eye justice. And much quicker justice than your arrests, your psychiatric evaluations, your arraignments, your trials, your appeals, *your goddam incompetent lawyer...* Live with that guilt forever? No! Jump! Slit! Blow your goddammed head off!

PETRA

Ach!

PETRA barges back into her unit. There is a brief silence, then:

JERRY
(Speaks loudly, so PETRA will be sure to hear him.)

We really have gotten off on the wrong foot here...Marcus is going to open the door... You won't want to miss this...

(Slight pause.)

Look, don't get me wrong. It's just that I put myself in other people's shoes and try to imagine what I would do in their situation. Lifelong habit. I'm empathetic. I mean, you go along, you try to be your best self, keep a lid on it... But you do something terrible, you accept the consequences, right? Take your medicine. Learn from your mistake, and move on... Of course some things you might do, well there's no lesson to be learned, right? "Oh, next time one of my kids acts up, I won't throw him off the roof." No. The guilt was too much. He couldn't forgive himself, and no mercy on earth could give him comfort. Same with the slitter. Couldn't forgive themselves. So they... Oh... Okay... You're right. They're unforgivable. I mean, if you can't forgive yourself...

PETRA emerges from her unit, looks at the closed door of unit 248.

PETRA

I thought you said Marcus opened the door.

JERRY

No. No. I said he's gone to get the master key so he can open the door. He'll be right back.

PETRA

Oh, for the love of—!

PETRA starts back into her space.

JERRY

Don't you want to be right here when we catch the bastard?

PETRA freezes, slowly turns to JERRY.

PETRA

What did you say? Catch… "the bastard?"

JERRY

Yeah.

PETRA

For your information, I've known a variety of bastards. Known them
well. Very well. So I don't award that title lightly. Okay?

JERRY

Okay…

PETRA

And we don't know a thing about him, do we? It is a him, isn't it? Isn't
he a "him?" He's a "he?"

JERRY

He… looked like a "he," I guess. But, it was so fast and so strange. The
hat. The hair. I'm usually pretty observant — lifelong habit — but…
Yeah, okay, I suppose he could have been a "she."

PETRA

Mm hmm. "He?" "She?" We don't even know his or her
gender, do we? Or is "He" or "She" a "Them?" Huh? So what else
could we possibly know about him or her…? Or them…? Hmm,
Mister Empathy?

JERRY

Okay, okay! Ya got me! Guilty! I'm a judgmental mental case! Lock
me up and throw away the key!

PETRA

Ach!

PETRA charges back into her unit. JERRY flips her the bird behind her back. The sound of a high electric whine is heard as MARCUS in the golf cart enters slowly from stage left.

JERRY

Halleluja!

(Shouts toward PETRA's unit.)

Hey! He's here! Marcus is here!

MARCUS and the cart roll past JERRY as MARCUS desperately attempts to stop the cart. PETRA emerges from her unit to watch. Just before MARCUS disappears stage right HE successfully halts the vehicle. HE puts it in reverse. With a "beep-beep-beep" the cart rolls back onto the stage and MARCUS manages to bring it to rest in front of JERRY and PETRA.

MARCUS

Sorry. Sorry about that.

JERRY

Well... all's well that ends well.

MARCUS

A problem play.

JERRY

With the cart?

MARCUS

What?

JERRY

Problem with the cart?

MARCUS

The play.

JERRY

The... play...?

MARCUS

All's Well That Ends Well.

JERRY

Yes. So it is.

MARCUS

Yes, a problem play. Neither comedy nor tragedy. Considered a
comedy originally, of course, but impossible to consistently stage
as such. Likewise impossible as tragedy. A problem. Never popular,
really, and for good reason: Mistaken identities, unjustifiable love
interests, clowns telling incomprehensible jokes—

JERRY

Are we still talking about the cart?

MARCUS

Oh. The cart? Oh. No. That's my fault. No problem with the cart.
Just the driver. I'm ashamed, really, that I haven't mastered the
operation of this machine. I can work The Boss's computer. I can
run my record player at home, and my high-fidelity system. I even
wired a lamp once. But... this machine! How is it that I can have the
mere thought to move from the office to a distant storage unit and
all I need do is settle into this comfortable seat, turn this key, press
down with my foot on this simple lever, and travel without further
effort through space and time? How is this possible?! Batteries!
Wires! Who conceived of these things? And — my god! — motors!
MOTORS! Motors with sufficient torque to carry my mass from office
to unit, and to do so on soft rubber wheels so that I — the driver,
the master — don't feel the bumps and irregularities of the road. I
am sitting upon millenniums of discovery and innovation — what
a piece of work is mankind, hmm? — and yet I cannot manage to
drive this thing. I have read the instruction book from cover to cover,
repeatedly; understood every word; enjoyed, even, the syntax of
excellent technical writing; yet when it comes to pushing the correct
lever or button at the appropriate time, I consistently fail. I am a big
disappointment to the hopes and dreams of every genius in history
who labored in the service of the human race... Ah, well. The ride

itself, when I do manage it, always thrills me. And, look! Although not gracefully, I have arrived successfully at my destination after all! Ta-daaa!

JERRY

Uh huh. Do you have the master key?

MARCUS

I have the master key.

JERRY

Then open the door! I'm telling you, this bast— this intruder, unlocked the vacancy lock, rolled up the door, ducked under and rolled the door back down again, even though it's, it's… still locked…

MARCUS

Difficult to imagine. But let us have a look.

MARCUS eases himself out of the golf cart and pulls a set of keys from his pocket. HE makes his way to the door of 248 as JERRY and PETRA maneuver themselves to better witness the reveal. MARCUS fumbles with the lock, drops the key on the ground, picks it up, drops it again. JERRY visibly grimaces in frustration. MARCUS recovers the key and again fiddles with the lock. It clicks. MARCUS removes the lock from the door and begins to roll it up. JERRY and PETRA stoop low to see under the slowly opening door and THEY rise from their stooped positions as the door itself rises to reveal — nothing. MARCUS, JERRY and PETRA (and audience) are staring at what appears to be an emptiness — a dark, cavernous room, with walls, ceiling and floor receding in deep perspective into a distant, gloomy, sad recess… (See Production Notes at end of play.*)

MARCUS (cont'd)

Nothing. Vacant. As I said.

In silence, THEY all stare for a moment longer at the void, then MARCUS lowers the door to the ground and locks it. (See Production Notes at end of play.*)

JERRY

I saw him. He, umm, she… them… *they!*… bowed, unlocked the door, opened it, went in, and closed it.

MARCUS

I believe you saw that. I can see it, the way you have described it, I can see it in my mind's eye:

(MARCUS demonstrates as he narrates the actions.)

This person walks past you as you sit before your box, labeled "Kate;" you call to them and they turns to you; and bows, like so… Then they turns toward the lock; releases it; rolls up the door partway; ducks beneath; and, as you say, enters the unit… "Nugacity." "Nu-gacity…" "Nugacity." Hmm. This word enters my mind just now. "Nugacity." Unbidden, it presents itself to me. Why? I have no idea. "Nugacity." This word has a meaning; I must have heard this word, or read it, somewhere. But what good does this word do me now? None. My mind teases me. Oh-ho, I have seen entire galaxies in a teacup. Does it happen to you? You say you saw someone enter two-forty-eight… and yet we saw no one.

JERRY

My mind isn't playing tricks on me, if that's what you mean. I'm a good observer — lifelong habit — and I saw someone go in there!

PETRA

Trick door.

JERRY

I know! Wait. What? What do you mean?

PETRA

There's something tricky about that door. And I don't know what you saw, but what I saw when it was open was not an empty unit.

MARCUS

Aha!

(Quotes, in French:)

"Ceci n'est pas une pipe."

(The word "pipe," in French, is pronounced as "peep.")

There is a brief silence, then:

JERRY

We had more than a peep. We had a good, long look, and the unit was empty.

PETRA

"Peep," Marcus?

MARCUS

I am seeing your point. "Ceci n'est pas une pipe." You are saying: "This is not a pipe." Correct? Magritte? Magritte's painting of a full-bent billiard smoking pipe? Which he inscribed: "Ceci n'est pas une pipe"…? "This is not a pipe"…? Magritte…?

PETRA

Oh! Yes! Yes! That's exactly what I'm saying. That was not an empty unit. It looked like an empty unit, but it wasn't an empty unit — an actual empty unit.

MARCUS

"Ceci n'est pas une… empty unit!"

PETRA

Yes!

MARCUS

"This is not an empty unit."

PETRA

Yes!

MARCUS

Might we say we saw a *representation* of an empty unit?

PETRA

Yes!

MARCUS

But not in itself an empty unit. It was an abstraction of Nothingness; a Something representing a Nothing.

PETRA

Yes!

MARCUS

Which would seem to indicate — that is to say, the *representation* of an empty unit which is in the unit itself, would seem to indicate that the unit is not actually empty.

PETRA

Yes!

JERRY

I'm lost.

PETRA

There is something going on in there. This man here—

    (SHE points at JERRY.)

—is right.

MARCUS

Jerry. His name is Jerry.

PETRA

Jerry is right.

JERRY

I am?

PETRA

There is someone in unit two-forty-eight.

JERRY

There is?

PETRA

Marcus, quick, open the door again. Let's catch the bastard.

MARCUS

Catch the bastard. Yes. Let's catch him. You say it was a "he," did you, Jerry? It's a "he?" He's a "he?" Not a "they?"

JERRY

Oh, hell, I don't know. Just open the goddammed door.

> *Again, MARCUS approaches the door of Unit 248 with his keys. Again he fumbles with the lock, drops his keys, fumbles again... Suddenly the sound of a ringing cell phone is heard. MARCUS, JERRY and PETRA simultaneously reach for their own cellphones. Apparently THEY have all programmed their phones' ringtones similarly. After a moment it is apparent that it is MARCUS's phone which is ringing. JERRY and PETRA replace their phones as MARCUS, with his finger, swipes the face of his ringing phone, lifts the phone to his ear.*

MARCUS

Hello?

> *(His phone rings again. HE pulls it from his ear, stares at it. It rings again. HE swipes it again with a finger and holds it to his ear.)*

Hello?

> *(His phone rings again. HE pulls it from his ear, stares at it. It rings again. HE swipes it again with a finger, and swipes it again, and again. Then he pokes at it, shakes it, swipes it, pokes it and shakes it. The phone rings no more... MARCUS holds it to his ear.)*

Hello...? Hello...?

> *(HE lowers the phone, looks at JERRY and PETRA.)*

I pushed the wrong button...

> *(HE looks again at the face of his silent phone*

The Boss's caller ID. I'd better go see what she wants.

PETRA

But—

MARCUS

She can be… Sometimes she can be… I'd better go see what she wants…

MARCUS returns the phone and keys to his pockets, gets into the waiting golf cart, looks over his shoulder, starts the cart and successfully manages to back the vehicle — "beep-beep-beeping" as it goes — off stage left. JERRY and PETRA watch as the beeping sound fades away, and dies…

PETRA

A-a-ach! For the love of—! What the heck is going on here?

JERRY approaches the lock on the door of 248 and reaches out his hand.

PETRA (cont'd)

No tampering with—

JERRY

I know!

(HE pulls his hand away.)

But, it has to be a trick lock or something. Right? I mean, what is he? They? Some kind of Houdini?

PETRA

Some kind of Illusionist?

JERRY

Some kind of Joker?

(Shouting at the door of 248.)

What are you?! Some kind of Joker?!

PETRA

What would be the point?

JERRY

There would be no point. To come here and — I don't know — to work a trick lock, or something? Why? To fool us, or something? Mess with our heads? What would be the point?

(Pounds on the door of 248. Shouts.)

What would be the point?!

PETRA

There would be no point.

JERRY

Right! There would be no point! And what about that, that, "peep" thing? What was that?

PETRA

I think it was some kind of painting.

JERRY

A— A painting? What?! A painting of the inside of an empty storage unit? What kind of a painting is that? Who would paint a thing like that? Is that art? Isn't art supposed to have a point?

(Again, shouting at the door of 248.)

Pointless!

(JERRY pounds the door once more. There is a brief silence.)

Come on, Marcus, get back here. I want some goddammed answers.

There is a brief silence. PETRA wraps her arms around herself, as if SHE felt a sudden chill, then SHE makes a move toward her storage unit.

PETRA

I need to find that box before it gets dark…

JERRY

Wait. Let's wait for Marcus. He'll be right back.

PETRA

I need that box.

JERRY

I'll help you later.

PETRA

You wouldn't be any help. It's too crowded in there. You'd just get in
my way. And I don't want anyone going through my personal stuff.

JERRY

I wouldn't "go through" anything. What do you think I am? A snoop?

PETRA

How would I know what you are? You may be a snoop for all I know.
Or worse.

JERRY

Well, I'm not, okay? I'm more like a… a Detective. I'm good at finding
things other people— "Worse?" Like what, for instance?

PETRA

I don't know.

JERRY

I'm just offering my help, that's all… Okay, look, try this: Describe it.
Out loud. Remind yourself. Sometimes that helps.

PETRA

I don't know… It's… It's a box, okay? Not an ordinary box — with
those flaps? It has its own lid. And it's printed with a design. Floral.
It's actually very pretty…

JERRY

Okay.

PETRA

Tied with a ribbon. A wide ribbon. Wide, with a sort of velvety sheen.
Rubbing it, you can feel the soft nub of the velvet with your thumb.
Green…? Green, I think. Like moss. A wide ribbon of mossy green
velvet that you can feel. I wish I could say it had a scent. It used to, I
think. I seem to remember it having a scent that comforted me. But
it's long ago faded away, I'm sure. If it still had a scent I would have
found it by now.

JERRY

You could just follow your nose!

PETRA

Yes! I would just let my sense of smell lead me to it. But everything smells of mustiness in there now. Mustiness and that mothball odor… Or was the scent I recall, actually the scent of mothballs?

JERRY

What's in it?

PETRA

Nothing. Stupid stuff…

JERRY

Pictures, I'll bet.

PETRA

Some.

JERRY

Diaries?

PETRA

No! No diaries.

JERRY

Scrapbooks?

PETRA

One.

JERRY

How big?

PETRA

Scrapbook size. Jeezus. You want exact measurements?

JERRY

No, the box. The box! (*Shouts.*) HOW BIG IS THE BOX?!

PETRA

(*Shouts back.*) I DON'T KNOW! LIKE A DRAWER! (*Quieter.*) A bottom drawer.

JERRY

Okay…

                         PETRA

That's what my mother called it.

                         JERRY

A drawer?

                         PETRA

Bottom. Bottom Drawer.

                         JERRY

Like in a chest of…?

                         PETRA

That's what she called a Hope Chest. Her words for it: a "Bottom
Drawer."

                         JERRY

Really? A Hope Chest? Let me guess: Filled with linens, silverware,
other useful items, heirlooms, some pictures — no diaries! — one
scrapbook-sized scrapbook, a formerly fragrant sachet, maybe, and
all wrapped and tied with a mossy-green velvet ribbon. Right? I'll be
damned… A Hope Chest.

                         PETRA

Lost. In all that junk…

                         JERRY

I can help you find—

                         PETRA

Didn't I already say?

                         JERRY

Right…

                         PETRA

"Jerry," is it?

                         JERRY

Yes. Yes! Jerry's the name!

        (HE extends his hand toward PETRA.)

And I have the pleasure of meeting…?

PETRA

Who is Kate?

JERRY

Kate?

PETRA
(Pointing at the bin, labeled "Kate," on the ground.)
Kate.

JERRY

Ah, yes, Kate. My ex-wife. Second… ex-wife. And your name is…?

PETRA

That's your ex-wife's — second ex-wife's — stuff?

JERRY

Uh huh.

PETRA
(Pointing at the cardboard box next to the bin.)
That, too?

JERRY

Yes. Well, actually, that? That box? No, that's… her.

PETRA

Her?

JERRY

Ashes… Her ashes…

PETRA

Oh. Eww! (*Points at the bin labeled "Rosalind."*)…and is Rosalind in there?

JERRY

No. Just some of her stuff.

PETRA

And Rosalind is…?

JERRY

My first ex-wife.

PETRA

And she is…?

JERRY

Alive. Still. Yes.

PETRA

And you're storing her stuff?

JERRY

It's stuff we had together. Shared stuff. I put it in storage when I remarried. Stuff I shared with Rosalind bothered Kate, so I just boxed it and put it away. The "Kate" boxes are stuff of Kate's I inherited.

PETRA

Bothered your third wife?

JERRY

There is no third wife.

PETRA
(Points into the open bin.)

Is that — was that — her gun?

JERRY

Kate's. Yes. I insisted she keep one. For protection…

PETRA
(Points again at the box containing the ashes.)

That's not a very nice box, considering what's in it. A plain cardboard box. Tied with string, not even a ribbon.

JERRY

That's how it came from the funeral parlor. When Kate die— pass— decea— crossed ov— passed aw— passed— Passed. When she PASSED, I was between homes… so I left her in her box. Her ashes.

PETRA

She didn't want them to be spread somewhere? Somewhere that meant something to her? To the both of you? Somewhere romantic?

JERRY

We never discussed things like that.

PETRA

Romance?

JERRY

Death… things.

PETRA

You never discussed something as important as her after-death wishes?

JERRY

No. Why would we?

PETRA

Well, when you get to be of a certain age, if you don't talk about such things, you're living in denial, don't you think?

JERRY

Of a certain age? My second ex-wife died at the age of forty-one.

PETRA

Oh. Oh! I just assumed… Sorry.

JERRY

Forty-one. And she was, at the time, at the age of forty-one, my ex-wife. EX. Wife. So why would we have discussed her after-death wishes, at the age of forty-one?

PETRA

No. Of course. You wouldn't have.

JERRY

No.

PETRA

She never re-married?

                    JERRY

No.

                    PETRA

Family?

                    JERRY

None.

                    PETRA

So, you took care of her final…

                    JERRY

Yes.

                    PETRA

Forty-one.

                    JERRY

Yes.

                    PETRA

Young.

                    JERRY

Yes.

                    PETRA

How long ago?

                    JERRY

Twenty-one years ago.

                    PETRA

You've had her in that, that, ugly box, for twenty-one years?

                    JERRY

Her ashes. Yes. I was… I've been… unsettled.

                    PETRA

How did she die?

                    JERRY

Accident.

PETRA

Oh. Sorry...

JERRY

You don't even know me, but you accuse me of things.

PETRA

What? What things?

JERRY

Being in denial.

PETRA

Sorry. I just assumed that—

JERRY

Exactly! I could assume a lot of things about you, too But I don't.

PETRA

What could you assume about me?

JERRY

Lots of things.

PETRA

Alright. Assume. Go ahead. Assume some things about me. I can't wait to hear them.

JERRY

Okay... You work hard...

PETRA

Go on...

JERRY

In some large institution...

PETRA

Okay...

JERRY

It's a grim job sometimes...

PETRA

Mm hmm…

JERRY

You live alone…

PETRA

Easy one.

JERRY

I assume you have never been married.

PETRA

Again, easy.

JERRY

You loved someone, but it turned bad.

PETRA

Happens to everyone.

JERRY

It hurt you.

PETRA

Brilliant, Mister Detective!

JERRY

Hurt so much you wished the person would die.

PETRA

People get angry.

JERRY

You fantasized about it…

(PETRA says nothing.)

In detail…

(PETRA says nothing.)

Traffic accident, maybe… Heart attack… Or maybe you'd do it yourself. Some lethal substance, say, that you yourself brought home from work, from your large institution, say, and administered in some clever way…

(PETRA says nothing.)

But you wouldn't do that of course, because you could never forgive yourself, could you? Oh, no. You would have to administer self-punishment — take a dose yourself. Or dash your brains out against a wall… Turn your car into oncoming—

PETRA

I would never do that!

JERRY

I also assume you don't believe my second ex-wife died accidentally.

PETRA

What? That's ridiculous! Why would you assume that?

JERRY

The way you looked at me when I said "Accident." Your look accused me of dishonesty.

PETRA

My look?

JERRY

Don't think I don't notice.

PETRA

Jerry, that's absurd!

JERRY

In fact, you've been giving me disapproving looks ever since we met.

PETRA

I don't even know you. Why would I give you disapproving looks?

JERRY

That's what I'd like to know!

PETRA

You're sounding very paranoid.

JERRY

I may be paranoid, but I know a funny look when I see one.

PETRA

Maybe I have strabismus. Did you ever think of that?

JERRY

Strab—? What's that?

PETRA

A wandering eye. One eye looks this way, the other looks that way.

JERRY

Oh… Really? How did I miss that?

PETRA

Or maybe you just irritate the hell out of me. Your whole attitude. Your whole, "Look at me, I'm such an empathetic person — Look at me, I'm such a big expert — I'll tell you how to unlatch your door – I'll find your stuff for you — I can guess your whole life history – 'Fragrant sachet' — 'Funny looks!'"

JERRY

"Fragrant…?"

PETRA

And I don't, by the way.

JERRY

Don't what?

PETRA

HAVE A WANDERING EYE! I just made that up!

JERRY

You don't?

PETRA

NO! Can't you even tell?!

JERRY studies PETRA's eyes for a moment, shrugs.

PETRA (cont'd)

Ach!

PETRA turns and barges back into her unit. JERRY

surreptitiously makes a face and sticks his tongue out behind PETRA's retreating back. SHE disappears. JERRY is alone on stage. HE sighs, walks to the bin marked "Rosalind" that is still on the blacktop. HE stoops, grunts, lifts it, and carries it back into the recesses of his unit and disappears. Silence. A few seconds later, the door of 248 rattles slightly, then opens a few inches, then a few inches more, and a few inches more, and a foot more, and another foot more... Very slowly, an object begins to emerge from beneath the door. When it is about half-way out, an apparent shove from inside 248 fully ejects the object. It's a fairly large steamer trunk, covered with stickers from cruise ships, airlines, hotels, etc. which document the trunk's extensive travels. The door of 248 slowly closes. A brief silence, then JERRY emerges from his unit, looks at the door of 248, looks toward PETRA's unit, flips the bird. HE spots the steamer trunk, looks away, does a double-take. HE cautiously approaches the trunk, looks left and right, bends down, grabs a handle and drags the trunk downstage a bit, away from the door of 248. HE looks left and right again and over his shoulder at PETRA's unit, then carefully tests the latch on the upstage side of the trunk. It is unlocked. JERRY carefully opens the lid. HE rummages in the open chest, appears to have found an item of interest, fiddles with it... Suddenly a spring-loaded trick "snake" jumps into the air from the unseen item in JERRY's hands. HE shouts:

JERRY

AH! — FUCK ME!

HE holds up the can he had opened from which the "snake" sprang.

JERRY (cont'd)

Son of a—! What the hell...?

HE puts the can back in the trunk, rummages a bit more, pulls out another object, holds it up. It is a pair of "Groucho Marx" glasses with thick black eyebrows,

42

big rubber nose, and mustache attached to the heavy
black frames. HE turns the item over and over in his
hands, then puts it on his face. HE does his best to mimic
Groucho Marx's line from the old TV show:

JERRY (cont'd)
"Say the secret woid…" "Say the secret woid…"

Meanwhile, PETRA has emerged from her unit, spots
JERRY, walks up behind him:

PETRA
Who are you talking to?

Surprised, JERRY jumps, shouts:

JERRY
JEEZUS!

HE spins to face PETRA, who, taken by surprise by the
"Groucho" glasses, jumps, shouts:

PETRA
CHRIST!

JERRY and PETRA
(Simultaneously.)
You scared me!

JERRY puts the "Groucho" glasses back in the trunk and
lowers the lid.

JERRY
Don't sneak up on a guy like that!

PETRA
I thought you were talking to Marcus.

JERRY
No. Just…

PETRA

(Points at the steamer trunk.)

Rosalind or Kate?

JERRY

What?

PETRA

That trunk. Rosalind stuff? Kate stuff?

JERRY

No.

PETRA

Your stuff?

JERRY

No. It was… It was over there, by the door.

PETRA

Two-forty-eight?

JERRY

Yeah. I heard some noise and I thought maybe Marcus was back, so I came out to check… and this was just standing there.

PETRA

And you opened it?

JERRY

It wasn't locked.

PETRA

How did it get there?

JERRY

I don't— How should I know? I came out of my unit and there it was.

PETRA

This is crazy.

JERRY

You're telling me.

PETRA

What's in it?

JERRY *carefully opens the lid. THEY stand for a moment staring at the trunk's contents, then JERRY reaches in and pulls out:*

JERRY

His hat! Her— They's— Their— THE hat!

PETRA

Huh.

It is, indeed, the same black, wide-brimmed, feather-adorned, theatrical hat, seen on THE LODGER's head earlier in the play. JERRY turns the hat over in his hands for a moment then places it on his head, takes it off again and examines it, puts it back on his head. Then HE takes PETRA by the hand and leads her downstage. With a flourish, in imitation of THE LODGER's earlier gesture, JERRY bows deeply to PETRA, speaks in mangled French:

JERRY

Bon jewr, my dam! Com ez vuze? Tray bee-en?

PETRA

Jerry…! That's silly!

JERRY

"Zher-ry?" Who eez zis "Zher-ry?" I am Zorro, at your ser-veece!

PETRA

Zorro was Hispanic, Jerry, not French.

JERRY

I make-a my mark-a!

With great flair, with his fingertips, JERRY slashes an imaginary "Z" in the air in front of PETRA's chest. SHE steps back a bit.

PETRA

Jerry! Stop it!

> *JERRY stops, removes the hat, turns it over in his hands a bit, then places it on the plastic bin labeled "Kate." Meanwhile, PETRA has been rummaging in the trunk. SHE pulls out a pair of "Googly-eye" glasses, with huge bouncing eyeballs on springs. SHE puts them on, turns to JERRY just as he returns to the trunk.*

JERRY

Jeepers! Where'd you get those peepers?!

PETRA

They were in the trunk.

JERRY

I know. I meant…

PETRA

Oh… Right! *(Sings:)* "Jeepers, Creepers,"

JERRY

(Sings:) "Where'd ya get those Peepers?"

> *PETRA shakes her head to make the Googly-eyes bounce.*

JERRY (cont'd)

Ha haa!

> *(Retrieves the "Groucho" glasses, puts them on, mimics Groucho's line again.)*

"Say the secret woid and win a hundred dollahs…"

PETRA
(Shaking the Googly-eyes.)

"NUGACITY!"

JERRY

You said the secret woid! You win a hundred dollahs!

> *THEY laugh. Then grow silent, looking at each other still*

*wearing their joke eyewear. THEY chuckle again, grow
silent again. PETRA removes the Googly-eyes, JERRY
removes the Groucho glasses. THEY put the items back
into the trunk.*

PETRA

This is crazy.

JERRY

You're telling me.

PETRA digs into the trunk, pulls out a shiny black pair of:

PETRA

Tap shoes! Men's tap shoes!

*SHE clicks the shoes together, makes the taps sound,
experiments… Soon she gets a rhythm going. JERRY
reaches into the trunk and pulls out a ukulele. HE begins
to strum it in sync with PETRA's tap rhythm. HE may or
may not know how to form chords on the instrument, but
it doesn't stop him from singing:*

JERRY
(Sings:)

"Tiptoe, Through the window, By the window, That is where I'll be!
Come tiptoe, Through the tulips, With me!"

*PETRA continues to tap the shoes while JERRY, still
strumming the uke and singing, begins to improvise some
dance steps around PETRA and the steamer trunk.*

JERRY (cont'd)
"Oh, tiptoe, From the garden, By the garden, Of the willow tree, And
tiptoe, Through the tulips, With me!"

*THEY continue the tapping and dancing and singing,
alternating verses:*

PETRA
"Tiptoe, From your pillow, To the shadow, Of a willow tree—"

JERRY

"And tiptoe, Through the tulips, With me."

PETRA

"And if I kiss you, In the garden, In the moonlight,
Will you pardon me? And tiptoe, Through the tulips,
With me!"

JERRY and PETRA
(Together.)

"And if I kiss you, In the garden, In the moonlight,
Will you pardon me?"

(They improvise a Big Finish.)

"And tiptoe, Through the tulips, With me-e-e-e-e!"

Exhausted, THEY laugh at their mutual creation.

JERRY

Whew! Don't wanna get a heart attack.

PETRA

No. That wouldn't be good.

JERRY

You know that song!

PETRA

Of course. You... You can't really play the ukulele, can you?

JERRY

No. Well, actually—

PETRA

But you did pretty well! Coulda fooled me!

JERRY

Actually, I did play once. A little. Back in... school...
But...

PETRA

But...

JERRY and PETRA
(Simultaneously.)

That was fun.

JERRY

Yeah, it was…

PETRA returns the tap shoes to the trunk.

PETRA

This is crazy…

JERRY returns the ukulele to the trunk.

JERRY

You're telling me…

HE pulls out a small tin container, opens the lid. PETRA watches, recognizes what's in the container.

PETRA

Makeup. Greasepaint sticks.
          (Takes out a stick, partially unwraps it.)
Jet black.
          (Holds the stick near JERRY's face.)
We can remove it later.

JERRY

…Okay.

PETRA applies two broad black bands to JERRY's face, one under each eye, like on a football player's face, or a SWAT cop's. SHE makes as though to apply more, but JERRY backs away.

JERRY (cont'd)

That's enough.

PETRA

Okay.

SHE re-wraps the stick and puts it back in the container then back in the trunk. JERRY and PETRA both dig in the trunk. JERRY pulls out a wig of long flowing dark hair, puts it on, strokes the gorgeous locks. PETRA pulls out a small book, opens it, flips through the pages, reads something to herself, laughs out loud.

JERRY

What?

PETRA
(Reads aloud from the book:)

"My husband took an IQ test and the results came back negative."

JERRY laughs, PETRA does, too. SHE hands the book to JERRY.

PETRA (cont'd)

There's more.

JERRY
(Reads from the book)

"My wife started walking five miles a day when she turned 60; now she's 75 and I don't know where the hell she is!"

THEY laugh. JERRY hands the book back to PETRA.

JERRY (cont'd)

Do another.

PETRA
(Reads another:)

"Skeleton walks into a bar, says, 'Gimme a beer and a mop.'"

A beat, then SHE laughs. JERRY doesn't.

JERRY

Uh huh… And…?

PETRA

What?

JERRY

And...? What else?

PETRA

Nothing else. It says here these are "one-liners."

JERRY

But... I don't get it.

PETRA

"Skeleton walks into a bar, says, 'Gimme a beer and a mop.'"

JERRY

"...walks into...?"

PETRA

A bar. A skeleton, right? Picture it: Skeleton... Beer... *Mop*?

JERRY

Lemme see that.
                    (*Takes the book from PETRA.*)
Is that really what it says?

PETRA
               (*A little peeved.*)
Of course that's what it says. I know how to read...

JERRY
        (*Studying the text of the one-liner.*)
"Gimme..." "Gimme a beer..." "Gimme a beer and a mop." "Gimme a
beer and a..." "Gimme a beer..." "Gimme a beer and a mop." "Gimme
a beer and a—" Oh. OH! He drinks the beer, and it all sloshes out
of him onto the floor because he's a— So he has to— Okay! I get it!
That's funny!

PETRA

Finally.

JERRY flips a page, studies it for a second; then:

JERRY

Wanna do one together?

PETRA

A one-liner?

JERRY

No. A joke. With two people.

PETRA

I don't know. Let me see…

JERRY shows PETRA the page. She studies it for a second; then:

PETRA (cont'd)
(Begins to read aloud:)

"An eighty-year-old couple is having trouble remembering things, so they go to the doctor who tells them they should start writing things down to help them with their memory. They thank him and go home…"

JERRY takes up where PETRA left off:

JERRY

"Later that night while listening to the radio, the old man gets up from his chair, and his wife asks:"

PETRA

"'Where are you going?'"

JERRY

"'To the kitchen.'"

PETRA

"'Will you get me a bowl of ice cream?'"

JERRY

"'Sure.'"

PETRA

"'Maybe you should write that down so you don't forget.'"

JERRY

"'I can remember that. Ice cream.'"

PETRA

"'Well, I also want some strawberries with the ice cream. Maybe you should write that down.'"

JERRY

"'I don't need to. Ice cream with strawberries. I can remember that.'"

PETRA

"'But I also want whipped cream on top. I know you'll forget that, so you better write it down.'"

JERRY

"'I don't need to write that down,' he says with some irritation. 'I can remember that!' And he fumes into the kitchen.'"

PETRA

"After about twenty minutes he returns from the kitchen and hands his wife a plate of bacon and eggs…"

JERRY

"She stares at the plate for a moment then says…"

PETRA

"'You forgot my toast!'"

THEY laugh.

JERRY and PETRA
(Together.)

That's funny!

JERRY

You were good! That was good!

PETRA

You, too! You sounded just like an old man!

(THEY laugh, return the joke book to the trunk.)

I mean, what is this stuff?

(SHE begins to pull a multicolored silk scarf from somewhere in the trunk.)

It's all joke stuff.

(The scarf continues to come out in a long stream.)

Magic stuff.

(SHE continues to pull yard after yard of scarf from the trunk.)

JERRY

The shoes... The uke... The hat...

PETRA

Yeah... It's... It's show-business stuff! "Show-Biz." "Show-Biz" stuff... "Show"... "Biz"... "Show-Biz"...

The scarf finally plays out. PETRA gathers it all back up and stuffs it back into the trunk.

JERRY

I think it's his stuff. The guy in two-forty-eight. And it must be a guy, right? Those tap shoes were a man's.

PETRA

They were. But this isn't a man's...

(Pulls from the trunk an elaborate, ruffled, woman's Elizabethan collar, fastens it around her neck, reaches back into the trunk.)

And this isn't either...

(Pulls out a fancy Elizabethan woman's headdress, puts it on.)

JERRY

Wow... Wow... You look... Wow...

PETRA

Methinks.

JERRY

Dost thou?

                                PETRA

Aye.

        *JERRY retrieves the black hat, puts it on over the wig he's
        still wearing.*

                                JERRY

Alas! What light... breaks?

                                PETRA

Speak!

                                JERRY

Wherefore art thou?

                                PETRA

Approach and speak!

                                JERRY

Ah, fairest maiden, wherefore art thou?

                                PETRA

Wherefore am I what? What sayest thou?

                                JERRY

What?

                                PETRA

Wherefore am I what?

                                JERRY

Wherefore art thou? I don't see-est thou. Thy balcony... It be dark...
Wherefore ist thy balcony...?

                                PETRA

"Wherefore" means "Why."

                                JERRY

What sayest thou?

                                PETRA

"Wherefore" doesn't mean "Where." It means "Why."

                    JERRY
What, fair maiden?

                    PETRA
"Why!" Not "Where!" "Why!"

                    JERRY
What? Thou confuseth I.

                    PETRA
When they say "Wherefore," they mean "Why."

                    JERRY
Who?

                    PETRA
What?

                    JERRY
When who says "Wherefore?"

                    PETRA
The Shakespeare people.

                    JERRY
Why?

                    PETRA
Right.

                    JERRY
What?

                    PETRA
Right. "Wherefore" means "Why."

                    JERRY
Why would "Where" mean "Why?"

                    PETRA
"Where" doesn't mean "Why!"

JERRY

I thought you said—

PETRA

"WhereFORE!" "WhereFORE" means "Why!" Not "Where!"

JERRY

That makes no sense.

PETRA

It's Shakespeare!

JERRY

"Wherefore" should mean "Where."

PETRA

Well, it doesn't. "Whither" means "Where." "Whither art thou?" means, "Where are you?" But if you ask me, "Wherefore is thy balcony?" in Shakespeare, you're asking me, "Why is your balcony?" That's ridiculous. And if you ask me, in Shakespeare, "Wherefore art thou?" you're asking me, "Why are you?" "WHY ARE YOU?!" It's an absurd question! ABSURD! With no possible answer! "Why are you...?" It's like, like... *ZEN!*

JERRY

You don't need to get so angry!

Suddenly, from inside Unit 248, there comes a startling BOOM! The sound rattles the closed door. PETRA screams with fright:

PETRA

AH!

PETRA draws close to JERRY. Another BOOM! PETRA screams again:

PETRA (cont'd)

AH!

And a third BOOM! PETRA screams a third time:

PETRA (cont'd)

AAHH!

> *PETRA removes the Elizabethan collar and headdress and hastily replaces them in the trunk. JERRY removes the black hat and the wig. HE tosses the wig into the trunk and closes the lid. Still holding the black hat, HE grabs the .38 revolver from the "Kate" bin. PETRA and JERRY watch as the red door of 248 slowly begins to rise. Smoke, or fog, curls upward from beneath the rising doorway. PETRA and JERRY draw even closer to each other, almost touching. JERRY puts the hat back on his head and points the gun toward Unit 248. When the door is half open, the trunk, as if it were violently tugged with an attached wire, is jerked back into the void of the open unit and vanishes from sight. The door of 248 descends. JERRY and PETRA, inches apart, turn to face each other.*

PETRA (cont'd)

Oh my god.

JERRY

I know.

PETRA

It sucked that trunk into its mouth like a frog catching a fly! There's someone in there!

JERRY

Yes! Yes! That's what I'm saying! But why? What's he — she – THEY! — Dammit, WHAT IS THEY DOING?! Goddammit! (*Pounds on the door of 248.*) What are you doing in there?! Who are you?! What do you want? (*Pounds on the door.*) Why?! WHY ARE YOU—?! (*Shouts toward stage left.*) Marcus! (*Mutters.*) Where the hell are you, you stupid, nerd? (*Shouts.*) Marcus! MARCUS!

> (*Pounds violently on the door of 248*)

Come out of there, goddammit! I know you're in there!

> (*Shouts off stage left*)

MARCUS! Dammit! I hate this! I am so pissed off right
now I can't even see straight!

(Viciously pounding on the door of 248.)

Open the door, dammit! Open - this - goddammed - door!

PETRA

I'm finished here. This place is scaring me. And so are you right now, if
you want to know the truth. And put that gun away! Are you crazy?!

SHE turns to her unit and begins preparations to close it
up. JERRY still holds the revolver.

JERRY

What are you doing? You can't leave now.

PETRA

Excuse me?

JERRY

You're a witness.

PETRA

So what?

JERRY

You can't leave until Marcus shows up and we tell him what we saw.
The trunk. The door.

PETRA

You tell him. I'm going home.

JERRY

But, you need to corroborate the story. You're a material witness!

PETRA

I don't care.

JERRY

You don't care? Oh, that's— That's just—! Oh, that's—! You—! That's
so—! I just can't—!

PETRA

My goodness! Your entire vocabulary in one sentence! Bravo!

JERRY

You have stuff here! You have a stake in this!

PETRA

I have a headache, actually, and you're making it worse.

JERRY

Oh, that's good. That's really good. You don't feel well, so you're just gonna walk away.

(Parodies her, with great exaggeration:)

"Ooh, I don't like this anymore. I'm just going to wa-a-alk away. I'll just wa-a-a-a-alk away. Here I am, just wa-a-a-a-a-alking away. I'll just let this boob, here — this… JERRY, here — handle everything and I'll just wa-a-a-a-a-alk away!"

PETRA

Go on, say it. "Just Like A Woman?"

JERRY

Just like a quitter. A deserter. A faithless, deceiving, betraying, cheating… cheater.

PETRA

You're crazy. I'm done.

SHE pulls the door all the way down and begins to lock her unit. JERRY crosses to her and grabs her wrist.

JERRY

No.

PETRA

Get your hand off me!

JERRY

You can't leave yet.

PETRA

I can and I will.

JERRY

No.

PETRA

I said get - your - hand - off - me.

JERRY obeys.

PETRA (cont'd)

Now get away from me…

JERRY remains in place.

PETRA (cont'd)

Back away from me. Now!

JERRY obeys.

PETRA (cont'd)

This place isn't crazy enough but now I have to deal with you! And put that gun away!

JERRY
(As he tucks the gun into his waistband)

Sorry. I was out of line, I know. But—

PETRA
(Mimics him.)

"Sorry…" "Sorry…" You think that lets you off the hook? Behave like a Bastard, and then say, "Sorry," and I'm supposed to forgive you? Have mercy on you? "Sorry…" Is that what you said to Kate? Hmm? After the "Accident?" Hmm? "Sorry, Kate. Sorry about that. I didn't know it was load—" Oh my god… It WAS the gun, wasn't it? Oh, my god… Did you tell her you were sorry? Huh? "Sorry, second ex-wife, but if it's any consolation, I'll store your ashes in an ugly cardboard box in a musty, low-rent, self storage unit for the next twenty-one years. So sorry."

Suddenly JERRY turns away and rushes into the depths of
his unit, disappearing among the boxes and bins…

PETRA (cont'd)

Oh, for the love of—!

(SHE speaks loudly so JERRY will be sure to hear her.)

Jerry… Jerry! What…? Are you hiding…? Jerry! What…? Did I
hurt your feelings…? Jeezus, what I wouldn't give to go back to the
day when men didn't have feelings! Didn't express their feelings…
Who encouraged that behavior…? Who gave permission…? Oh, for
the— Jerry… Jerry! Come out of there. Look, it's, it's this place — this
freaky… door! I'm more than a little bit terrorized, I'll admit…

(Quieter. More to herself than to JERRY.)

I'm not even sure if I remember whether I put that box in here or
just left it behind somewhere. I don't have a clear picture anymore.
And that's not exactly reassuring. I'm panicking a little… And you
did bully me, Jerry. You can't do that to a woman. Not this woman!
You hurt me… But I shouldn't have— Oh, sometimes I'm so horrible.
Okay, I accept your apology… I have hurt you, haven't I? Oh my
god—I know I have. I'm horrible… Did you really do that, though?
Did you actually shoot her? That's so sad. How could you forgive
yourself? But a gun in the house, you know… The statistics on that…
Was it a fight, or…? I'm sorry, I'm sorry, I shouldn't ask! I don't even
know you. I'm a horrible person. Jerry…?

A pause… then JERRY calls from within his unit:

JERRY

I'm coming out…

PETRA

Alright…

JERRY
(From within.)

Don't look at me when I do.

62

PETRA

…alright…

(SHE turns her back to JERRY's unit.)

I'm not looking now…

JERRY
(From within.)

Okay, then… I'm coming out…

PETRA

Come out, then. I'm not looking…

JERRY
(From within.)

I'm coming out…

Still wearing the hat, and with the .38 revolver in hand,
JERRY emerges from his unit. HE's wiping his eyes with
his free hand.

PETRA

Are you out?

JERRY sighs deeply. HE wipes his eyes again, sniffles,
wipes his nose, wipes his eyes again. HE sighs, goes silent…
After a moment, PETRA speaks:

PETRA (cont'd)

Are you okay?

JERRY raises the gun…

PETRA (cont'd)

Can I turn around?

…and JERRY lowers the gun into the "Kate" bin.

PETRA (cont'd)

Won't you please say something?

                    JERRY

No.

                    PETRA

No?

                    JERRY

No.

   PETRA turns to face JERRY.

                    PETRA

NO?

                    JERRY

No.

                    PETRA

Please?

                    JERRY

No.

                    PETRA

That's it?

                    JERRY

Yes.

                    PETRA

And nothing else?

                    JERRY

Nothing.

                    PETRA

Ever?

                    JERRY

Ever.

                    PETRA

Why not?

JERRY
(Shrugs.)

Wherefore?

JERRY and PETRA stand face-to-face — a silent pair of dead stone statues. Then the whining sound of the electric golf cart is heard.

PETRA
He's here! He's here! OH, THANK CHRIST! MARCUS IS HERE!

MARCUS manages to pull his cart to a stop.

PETRA (cont'd)
Marcus! Marcus, you won't believe—

MARCUS waves his hand at PETRA, signaling her to be quiet. MARCUS remains on the seat of the golf cart. HE closes his eyes and begins to sway.

PETRA (cont'd)
Marcus?

MARCUS does not respond. HE begins to utter small moans as HE sways, eyes still unopened.

PETRA (cont'd)
Marcus? Are you alright?

JERRY
What's the matter with him?

PETRA
I'm calling Nine-One-One…

PETRA searches for her cellphone. MARCUS begins to heave his shoulders and writhe and shudder and make almost orgasmic sounds. JERRY shakes MARCUS, shouts:

JERRY
MARCUS!

MARCUS opens his eyes and waves his hand at JERRY,
as if to signal "Hush!" JERRY backs away. MARCUS,
still holding up his hand, again closes his eyes, becomes
still, hunches up his shoulders, shivers… and then relaxes
completely, drops his hand into his lap, and is still.

JERRY (cont'd)

My god. Marcus…?

HE cautiously advances toward MARCUS. Just as JERRY
is about to touch him, MARCUS opens his eyes and pulls
a small pair of wireless earbud earphones from his ears,
wipes a tear or two from his eyes. PETRA abandons her
call, approaches MARCUS.

MARCUS

Debussy. Of course. One finds it difficult to disagree with those who
say *Claire de Lune* is the most beautiful piece of music ever written.
Gives me chilblains every time I hear it. Infallibly. I love Brahms, but
Debussy… *Girl With The Flaxen Hair*… Ahhh…

(He indicates the earbuds.)

At the dentist last year they showed me how these work. Noise-
blocking. Since acquiring them I use them to do just that: block
noise. Especially here. The trucks that come in, the scraping of the
doors rising and lowering… But whenever I meet with The Boss,
afterward, I open my cellular phone and listen to music. At the
dentist last year for a root canal they asked me what music I would
like to listen to. Imagine! Music! During a root canal operation!
"Well," I said, "some Corelli would be wonderful." The dental
assistant was unfamiliar with Corelli, apparently, and suggested
smooth jazz was a particular favorite of root canal patients. I
apologized for suggesting an obscure Baroque composer, saying
I had just spoken off the top of my head, and that I might be able
to tolerate smooth jazz as an alternative to the sound of dental
instruments at work inside my head. However, the dentist suggested
searching for the word "Corelli" on his cellular phone, and I will
be darned if they didn't find a source of Arcangelo Corelli's better-
known works! So I listened to Corelli throughout the procedure.
Wonderful! Although, I did detect at least two Vivaldi's among

the Corelli's, and I think there was also a Telemann, but I couldn't be sure of that because by that point the noise of the little sawing instrument they use to kill the nerve and scrape it out of the tooth canal overcame the noise-blocking properties of the ear devices. Sound is conducted very efficiently through bone, you know. Much more efficiently than through the air.

JERRY

Marcus, Jeezus, listen to me. You are going to lose a couple of renters if you don't investigate this situation in two-forty-eight. Right now! We're demanding it!

MARCUS

Oh. Yes. There is some interloper in there, you say.

JERRY

Yes! And a, a chest of some kind. It appeared in front of the door and—

PETRA

A trunk. A trunk full of Magic things, and—

MARCUS

Magic things?!

PETRA

Joke things, and—

MARCUS

Joke things?!

JERRY

Hats. And wigs.

PETRA

Show Biz Things.

MARCUS

Show Biz Things?!

JERRY *grabs the black hat from his head.*

JERRY

This was in it! It's his. He's a "he"! It's his hat! The guy who went in there! It was in that trunk!

MARCUS

And where is this Magic Trunk full of Show Biz Things?

PETRA and JERRY exchange glances, then:

PETRA

It got… sucked back into the unit.

MARCUS

Like… Magic?

PETRA

That door opened by itself and the trunk just vanished!

MARCUS

And where had the trunk come from?

JERRY

I found it in front of two-forty-eight, and it wasn't there before.

MARCUS

So it appears to have appeared?

JERRY

Yes!

PETRA

And then it disappeared. Right into two-forty-eight. And there was smoke coming out!

MARCUS

Smoke?

PETRA

Smoke!

JERRY

Or, like, I don't know, like — it smelled like party fog. Like from one of those, you know, party foggers?

                    PETRA
Whatever! There's something weird going on behind that door!

                    JERRY
Open it, Marcus. You'll see.

                    PETRA
Open it.

                    MARCUS
I am forbidden.

        There is a pause. Then…

            JERRY and PETRA
                (Together.)
What?

                    PETRA
Forbidden?

                    MARCUS
As I said.

                    JERRY
Who? Who forbids?

                    MARCUS
She. The Boss.

                    PETRA
Didn't you tell her what's going on in there?

                    MARCUS
I did happen to mention, in the course of my just-concluded conference with her, that someone is alleged to have entered two-forty-eight and appears to be occupying it in violation of contractual terms, and she replied as follows:
            (Mimics the voice of The Boss:)
"Two-forty-eight is a vacant unit locked with a standard vacancy lock. No one can enter two-forty-eight without the master key. Only you—" meaning me "—and I—" meaning she "—have a master key.

Therefore two-forty-eight is by definition, and will continue to be until such time as it is rented, A Vacant Unit. And it will remain locked. Questions…? No…? Then you are dismissed. Now give your Mother a kiss."

JERRY

Your…?

PETRA

Mother…?

MARCUS

I needed income. The job was available.

PETRA

Your mother.

MARCUS

I think I know what you are thinking: Ninety. Her ninetieth birthday occurs next month. She is… sturdy.

JERRY

So… you're saying you won't — you may not — open two-forty-eight?

MARCUS

Correct. I am forbidden.

PETRA

But doesn't she care about what's happening in her own facility?

MARCUS

Her cares are many.

PETRA

Then why does she forbid you?

MARCUS

Her ways are mysterious.

PETRA

Call her, Marcus! Tell her you're here at the unit and renters are angry. She'll change her mind.

MARCUS

Her work day is done. Her phone will not ring.

PETRA

Then go get her, for Heaven's sake! Let her see for herself!

MARCUS

She has left the premises.

PETRA

Jeezus, Marcus!

JERRY

Open that door!

MARCUS

I may not.

JERRY

Marcus! Dammit! Grow some balls, why don't you?!

MARCUS

What, exactly, does that mean? "Grow some balls." In a literal sense, it's absurd. And as metaphor, the premise is—

JERRY

It means don't be such a Mama's Boy! Okay? It means grow up! It means get your head out of the clouds and your comic books and your novels and your Picture Books and join the real world. It means quit your goddam "Gee whiz - What a wonderful world - Corelli - Debutini – Claire the Luna" bullshit and grow some balls! You don't need your mother to tell you what to do. Make your own decisions!

MARCUS

But, I have.

JERRY

Open the door!

MARCUS

I have made the decision to obey The Boss and leave it closed and locked.

PETRA

Marcus, listen to me: Suppose someone comes into the yard right now and wants to rent a unit, and two-forty-eight is the only vacancy. Wouldn't you allow that person to inspect the unit?

MARCUS

Of course I would. That is part of my job.

PETRA

Alright, then, I want to rent another unit. May I please inspect two-forty-eight?

There is a slight pause, then:

MARCUS

No.

PETRA

But I want to rent it.

MARCUS

But you don't.

PETRA

But I do.

MARCUS

But I know you don't.

PETRA

How do you know?

MARCUS

Any reasonable person would understand that in these circumstances you are constructing a fiction to excuse me from carrying out The Boss's wishes. I am a reasonable person. Reasonable enough to know you don't intend to rent another unit.

PETRA

Yes, I do!

MARCUS

No, you don't.

                    PETRA

I do!

                    JERRY

She does!

                    MARCUS

She doesn't.

                    PETRA

Then I want to move out!

                    MARCUS

You just paid six months in advance.

                    PETRA

I want my money back!

                    MARCUS

Of course. But there will be a substantial penalty. It's in the contract.
Shall we do the paperwork? Will you be out today?

                    PETRA

No! I couldn't possib—! There's too much—! Jerry?!

                    JERRY

Marcus, listen, there may be civil issues here. Criminal issues. Code
violations. Legal liabilities. *Homeland* issues, if you catch my drift. I
mean, the door opened and there was smoke, or fog, or something,
pouring out of there!

                    MARCUS

The door opened by itself.

               JERRY and PETRA
                  (Together.)

Yes!

                    MARCUS

And this Magic Trunk full of Show Biz things vanished — sucked
right into the unit.

JERRY and PETRA
(Together.)

Yes!

MARCUS

And you wish me to open the door of two-forty-eight and investigate the unit for potential Homeland issues.

JERRY and PETRA
(Together.)

Yes!

MARCUS

I am forbidden.

JERRY

MY GOD, Marcus!

PETRA

What's wrong with you?!

MARCUS

Well, I am too diffident. I am socially inept. I am not half the man my father was. I am missing many teeth, and those remaining are unsound. I have benign prostate hyperplasia. My eyes are weak. I live in my Mother's basement. My bodily odors are unpleasant. I always tell the truth. I cannot drive a golf cart well. I don't know the definition of "synecdoche" but am too lazy to look it up. I—

JERRY slaps MARCUS.

PETRA

Jerry!

MARCUS staggers backwards a few steps, actually turns his other cheek. JERRY slaps MARCUS again.

PETRA (cont'd)

JERRY!

JERRY

Dammit, Marcus—! I'm sorry. But you have to take this seriously!

MARCUS

You asked a question. I took it seriously.

PETRA

The *situation*, Marcus. You have to take this *situation* seriously.
Marcus, listen to me: Think about your mother for a minute. Your
mother… It's obvious that you respect her. I admire that in you. And
you must love her very much, too. Don't you, Marcus? Don't you love
your mother very, very much?

MARCUS

(He is holding both hands to his reddened cheeks as he answers.)

Yes…

PETRA

You take good care of her?

MARCUS

Yes…

PETRA

Of course you do. You're a loving, caring, son. What if there's a fire
in there? Think how it would hurt her if this whole place went up
because you didn't investigate. Ninety years old! How could she bear
the loss? At that age…? Your father left all this to her?

MARCUS

He did…

PETRA

He worked hard to build this place up so you and your mother would
have something after he was gone, right?

MARCUS

Yes…

PETRA

How would your poor mother, your poor ninety-year-old mother, feel
if all her husband's hard work went up in smoke?

MARCUS
(Holding back tears.)

Bad...

PETRA

What kind of a son would let that happen to his mother...?

MARCUS
(Wiping at tears.)

I don't know... A bad son...

PETRA

And you're not a bad son, Marcus. You're a good son. Open the door, Marcus. For your mother's sake...

There is a slight pause as MARCUS wipes away the last of his tears, takes a deep breath, then:

MARCUS

My mother trusts me to obey her wishes. I am Trustworthy. She would have me no other way than to be Trustworthy. You wouldn't either, would you? Of course you wouldn't. And so, I am forbidden. And so, I shall not.

PETRA

This is ridiculous!

JERRY

Open that door, Marcus.

PETRA

Yeah, Marcus, open that goddamned door.

MARCUS

Please have empathy. You know I can't carry out your wishes.

JERRY

Oh, it's not a wish anymore, Marcus. It's an order.

MARCUS

I don't understand how I would be compelled to follow an order from you.

JERRY digs into the "Kate" bin and retrieves the .38 revolver, points it at MARCUS.

> JERRY

This is how you're compelled.

> PETRA

Jeezus, Jerry…

> MARCUS

A firearm?

> JERRY

Smith and Wesson thirty-eight.

> MARCUS

Was that in storage in your unit?

> JERRY

It was.

> PETRA

Jerry…

> JERRY

It's allowed by the rules. You know that.

> PETRA

Jerry…

> JERRY

Now open that door!

> PETRA

Jerry. Don't do this…

> JERRY
> *(Swings the gun toward PETRA.)*

Stop calling me Jerry.

> PETRA

I'm calling the Police!
> *(She does not move.)*

MARCUS

It is allowed by the rules to store certain firearms, yes. But storage of
live ammunition is not allowed. Since I began work here I have come
to know you, Jerry, as a rule-abiding renter. So I believe I am correct to
assume that the weapon you hold is not loaded with live ammunition…

ALL THREE stand still for a moment. Silence. Then
JERRY lowers the revolver.

PETRA

Put it away, Jerry.

JERRY

Stop calling me Jerry!

JERRY puts the .38 back into the "Kate" bin.

PETRA

Okay, Marcus, you win. We understand. Right, Jerry? We accept that
you can't open that door, and we don't want you to disobey your
mother.

MARCUS

Thank you! Thank you!

PETRA

So here's what can happen: Let us do it. Let us open the door.
Technically, you won't have betrayed anyone's trust. See?

MARCUS

But you can't open it. The door is locked.

JERRY
(Catching on.)

Right. Right! But if we have the master key, then we can unlock the
door ourselves.

PETRA

Then we can get some answers, and you won't be guilty of
anything. You could, you know, maybe, drop the key, or something.
Accidentally…

MARCUS

On Purpose… "Accidentally On Purpose," as they say.

JERRY

Yeah.

PETRA

Or, I don't know — one of us could take it from you, when you're not looking, or…

There is a slight pause. Then:

MARCUS

I believe you both know how I must answer you.

Suddenly PETRA leaps at MARCUS and grabs him by his wrist.

PETRA

Grab him, Jerry!

JERRY obeys PETRA. THEY stretch MARCUS's arms out wide.

PETRA (cont'd)

Get his keys!

JERRY

I don't know where they are!

PETRA

Where are they, Marcus.

MARCUS

I can't tell you that.

JERRY

Dammit, Marcus, where are your keys?!

MARCUS

Can't say.

JERRY

For Christ's sake, Marcus, you're in danger! I threatened you with
a weapon! That's assault with a deadly weapon! We're manhandling
you! That's Battery! Nobody can blame you if you give us your keys?!

MARCUS

Can't.

JERRY

Dammit!

> *Still holding MARCUS by a wrist, JERRY begins to
> swipe at MARCUS's pockets — those HE can reach —as
> MARCUS does his best to elude JERRY.*

PETRA

Jeezus, Marcus, hold still!

> *Now PETRA, still holding MARCUS by a wrist, also begins
> to swipe at MARCUS's pockets — those SHE can reach —
> as MARCUS does his best to elude PETRA. The struggle
> evolves into a piece of comic choreography. JERRY and
> PETRA tangle with MARCUS and with each other, groping
> each other's clothing and occasionally, inappropriately, each
> other. THEY curse and bicker throughout, and the black hat
> is knocked off of JERRY's head.*

JERRY

Dammit, Marcus!

PETRA

Jerry, that's my ass!

JERRY

Sorry!

PETRA

Give me those keys!

JERRY

Ouch, for Christ's sake!

PETRA

I can't see anything!

JERRY

Get your finger out of my—

MARCUS
(Pleading.)

Please! These are my only work clothes. Please don't damage them.

*Suddenly furious, JERRY pulls hard at MARCUS's arm—
so hard that PETRA loses her grip on MARCUS. JERRY
grabs MARCUS by the lapels of his workshirt, pushes him
around the stage while screaming into MARCUS's face.*

JERRY

Shut up! SHUT UP! You bastard!

PETRA
(Following JERRY and MARCUS, screaming at MARCUS.)

Twit!

JERRY

Goody two-shoes!

PETRA

Know-it-all!

JERRY

Nancy Boy!

PETRA

Prissy Pants!

JERRY

Nerd face!

PETRA

Wimp!

JERRY

Jerkoff!

PETRA

Jagoff!

JERRY

Fairy!

PETRA

Twerp!

JERRY

FAGGOT!

*Suddenly MARCUS loses his balance and falls —right
on top of the cardboard box tied with string. The box
explodes, Kate's ashes erupt, like a volcano, from beneath
the prone MARCUS. PETRA screams:*

PETRA

AAHHH!

JERRY

NO-O-O! NO-O-O-O-O-O!

MARCUS

I'm sorry.

JERRY

KA-A-A-ATE!

(Stoops and grabs MARCUS by the front of his workshirt.)
You son of a bitch!

*JERRY hauls MARCUS to his feet and shoves
MARCUS backwards, slamming him hard into the
door of 248.*

PETRA

Jerry! You're hurting him!

JERRY

Now look what you've done, you son of a whore! My Kate is
everywhere!

(Still holding him by the lapels, he slams MARCUS hard into the door.)

Everywhere!

Again JERRY slams MARCUS into the door.

PETRA

Jerry! Stop it!

JERRY

You useless piece of shit!

Once more, JERRY slams MARCUS against the door. PETRA screams:

PETRA

JERRY, LET HIM GO!

JERRY lets MARCUS go. MARCUS, limp, face bloodied, slides down and comes to rest, motionless, propped against the door of 248.

PETRA (cont'd)

My god, Jerry. What have you done?

Suddenly the door of 248 moves a bit. A gap appears beneath the door.

JERRY

Holy crap.

The door rises a bit more; a bit more; and still more. MARCUS's limp body, no longer supported by the opening door, slumps backward into the opening unit. JERRY backs away, joins PETRA as they both observe what the finally fully opened door reveals:

PETRA

… Nothing.

JERRY

… Nothing.

> *There is nothing. Bare concrete block walls and bare concrete floor. (See Production Notes at end of play.*)*

PETRA

Should we check it out?

JERRY

I'm not going in there!

PETRA

No. Me either…

JERRY

The door…

PETRA

Yes.

JERRY

How did it…?

MARCUS
(From his prone position on the floor.)

I must not have locked it properly.

JERRY

Oh, shit!

PETRA

Marcus!

> *PETRA and JERRY rush to MARCUS, help him to sit up.*

JERRY

I am so sorry, Marcus!

PETRA

Oh, my God, Marcus! Oh, I'm a horrible person!

                    JERRY

Jesus, I really hurt you. I'm so, so sorry!

                    PETRA

I'll call Nine-One-One.

                    MARCUS

No.

                    JERRY

Are you in pain, Marcus?

                    MARCUS

Yes.

                    JERRY

We'll call the rescue.

                    MARCUS

No.

                    PETRA

No?

                    MARCUS

No. They'll question me. They'll question you.

                    PETRA

Of course they will.

                    JERRY

It's procedure.

                    PETRA

We'll take what comes. Right, Jerry?

                    JERRY

Right.

                    MARCUS

No.

                    JERRY

Marcus—

                    MARCUS
Help me to stand. Please?

                    PETRA
Are you sure?

                    MARCUS
Yes.

                    PETRA
Alright...

        PETRA and JERRY help MARCUS to his feet.

                    JERRY
Okay? Are you okay?

                    MARCUS
Yes.

        (Unsteady, he takes a careful step forward. Suddenly
        his ankle gives out under him and he muffles a sharp
        cry of pain.)
Mmff!

        PETRA grabs MARCUS to support him.

                    PETRA
Marcus, you need medical attention. You may have a concussion, or
worse. I know what I'm talking about.

                    MARCUS
            (Extricating himself from PETRA's support.)
I'll be alright.

                    PETRA
I'm going to call Nine-One-One.
                    (She does not move.)

        MARCUS, favoring his hurt ankle, carefully turns,
        examines the open, empty unit 248.

86

MARCUS

… Nothing…

JERRY
(Also looking at the empty unit.)

… Nothing…

PETRA
(Also looking at the empty unit.)

… Nothing…

MARCUS

The door. I hit it. Jarred it.

JERRY
(Ashamed.)

I did that. Jeezus. I pushed you against it. Over and over. Hard.

MARCUS

I must not have locked it properly. Don't tell Mother. Please?

JERRY

Of course I won't. But, oh, Marcus, I'm so sorry. I'm an animal.

MARCUS

I forgive you.

PETRA

I started it. I tackled you! What's wrong with me? Oh, I'm a horrible
person.

MARCUS

I forgive you.

PETRA

How can you say that?

MARCUS

It's in my nature.

JERRY

I can't accept that.

MARCUS

My nature?

JERRY

Your forgiveness.

MARCUS

But, that is my nature.

PETRA

Marcus, no. You—

MARCUS

You have apologized to me and I have accepted your apologies. Please accept my forgiveness.

MARCUS, favoring his bad ankle, turns to the door of 248 and begins to roll it down.

PETRA

Alright. Alright. Thank— Thank you, Marcus.

JERRY

Thank you, Marcus.

MARCUS

My pleasure.

MARCUS begins to lock the door of 248.

JERRY

We'll buy you some new work clothes, Marcus.

PETRA

Yes! Yes! It's the least we can do.

MARCUS stops, examines his torn work clothes, turns to JERRY and PETRA.

MARCUS

You will?

                              JERRY

Yes.

                              PETRA

Of course we will.

                             MARCUS

Thank you! Thank you so much!

        MARCUS shakes JERRY's and PETRA's hands in turn.

                              PETRA

You're welcome!

                              JERRY

You're welcome!

        *MARCUS completes the locking procedure as HE
        continues speaking.*

                             MARCUS

I am so grateful to you! These are the only work clothes I own. Oh,
thank you! Thank you! Um… The Boss prefers we wear Dickies
Brand. Would that be alright?

                              JERRY

Dickies… Yes.

                              PETRA

Of course. No problem.

                             MARCUS

Thank you!

        (MARCUS tests the lock to make sure it's secure.)

There. That seems right. And… may I ask one more favor? Could you
help me to the cart, please? It's late. I need to punch out. And my ankle—

                              PETRA

Yes!

                              JERRY

Of course!

JERRY and PETRA support a limping MARCUS as THEY help him into the golf cart.

MARCUS

Oh, and… Size Medium.

PETRA

Size…?

MARCUS

Medium.

JERRY

Medium?

MARCUS

Yes, please. My Dickies…?

JERRY

Your work clothes!

MARCUS

Yes. Medium. Khaki.

JERRY

Of course! Yes! No problem!

MARCUS

Oh, and one last thing, sorry. The hat…? Perhaps I should take it with me…? For evidence?

JERRY

Yes. Of course.

JERRY retrieves the black hat and hands it to MARCUS who puts it on his head and adjusts it.

MARCUS

Thank you.

JERRY

You're welcome.

*MARCUS turns the cart key, waves at JERRY and PETRA
who wave back. MARCUS looks over his shoulder and...
the cart rolls forward. JERRY and PETRA jump out of the
way. MARCUS stops the cart.*

MARCUS

Sorry. So sorry.

PETRA

That's alright!

JERRY

No problem!

*MARCUS takes a deep breath, looks over his shoulder,
starts the cart, and it successfully backs off stage, "beep-
beeping" as it goes. MARCUS, smiling, gives a quick
"thumbs up" sign to PETRA and JERRY just before HE
disappears. MARCUS is gone. There is a brief silence. Then:*

PETRA

It's getting dark. I have to straighten up in there and...

JERRY

Yeah. Yeah. I need to... to sweep up... Kate.

PETRA

Okay. Well...

PETRA turns to her unit, opens up the door.

JERRY

Okay...

PETRA

Okay...

*SHE disappears into her unit. JERRY looks over his
shoulder toward where MARCUS disappeared, then
cautiously walks to the door of 248. HE reaches his hand
toward the lock, hesitates, then grabs it, shakes it, fiddles
with it, tries to open the door. HE can't. HE gives up,*

collects a broom and dust pan from his unit, sweeps up
some of the scattered ashes, and dumps them into the
damaged cardboard box. HE puts the cardboard box
into the "Kate" bin on the ground, stares into the bin for
a moment, then pulls out the .38 revolver. HE stands up,
turning the revolver over and over in his hands. Then
PETRA calls from within her unit:

PETRA
(From within.)

Jerry?

    JERRY quickly hides the gun behind his back. Calls
    back to PETRA:

JERRY

Yes? What?

PETRA
(From within.)

Jerry, I could use your help. I think I see something, but I can't reach it.

JERRY

I— Sure. Okay.

    HE starts toward PETRA's unit, hesitates, looks at the gun
    for a moment.

PETRA
(From within.)

Jerry?

    JERRY tucks the gun into his waistband.

JERRY

Yup. Coming.

        HE disappears into PETRA's unit.

PETRA
(From within.)

"Petra."

JERRY
(From within.)

What?

PETRA
(From within.)

My name. My name is "Petra."

JERRY
(From within.)

Oh. Petra. Nice to meet you.

> *There is silence for a moment. The stage is growing
> darker. The shaded lights positioned over each unit
> flicker on. The red door of 248 glows under the light,
> as though it were a grand, velvet, spotlit Act Curtain
> in some majestic theater. Suddenly, slowly, the door
> of unit 248 begins to open. When it is maybe a third
> of the way up, THE LODGER, stooping under the
> door to clear it, emerges. HE rolls the door back down
> and appears to lock it. HE turns to face the audience,
> looks at the audience for a moment, and then, in
> the spotlight effect, executes a deep, theatrical bow,
> sweeping the ground with his hat — THE hat —
> exactly as HE had bowed to JERRY earlier in the play.
> HE returns upright after his bow and begins to exit
> stage right. Suddenly his ankle gives out under him
> and he muffles a sharp cry of pain:*

THE LODGER
Mmmff!

> *HE continues to exit stage right, gingerly, carefully,
> painfully. His halting gait uncannily echoes MARCUS's
> limping steps the last time we saw him… HE is gone.*
>
> *JERRY emerges from PETRA's unit. HE has heard the
> THE LODGER's cry. HE looks toward stage right. Then:*

PETRA
(From within.)

Jerry…?

JERRY

Coming…

> *HE pulls the revolver from his waistband, enters PETRA's unit.*

PETRA
(From within.)

Jerry…?

JERRY
(From within.)

Petra…?

> *A beat… Blackout.*

END OF PLAY

*Production Notes:

—When we first see the "interior" of the fully opened Unit 248, it could very well be, as PETRA suggests, a painting, a representation of an empty storage unit. It need not be realistic. The audience should feel that some theatrical effect is being presented to them; only JERRY, in the play, seems to immediately take the representation at face value.

—Any further reveals of Unit 248's empty interior can be as realistic as the director and designer wish.

—248's lock, of course, only seems to lock…

THE OCCUPANT

"Median Home Price Drops…
$825K Median home price in June in San Diego County"
— *San Diego Union-Tribune*, July 19, 2022

CASTING VARIATIONS

I'm always in favor of a director having final choice in casting a play. But for THE OCCUPANT, I have specified the character JUNE as Black, and the characters GINA, JAMES and JOE as White. No overt issues of race are explored in the play; however — especially in an era of intense focus on equity, diversity, and inclusion — casting characters specifically by race bears significant subtext, and rightfully so.

I propose, therefore, that THE OCCUPANT offers a unique opportunity for an adventurous producer and/or director to mount a double-bill — either as a matinée/evening presentation, or two consecutive evening performances — featuring variations in racial casting. Contrasting back-to-back performances, I suggest, can give audience members of any race an occasion to examine, or discover, their own implicit biases. Perhaps a matinée features the original, suggested racial casting, while an evening performance features the same play but with GINA and JUNE as White and JAMES as Black, for instance — or other variations a producer or director may imagine.

THE OCCUPANT

Cast of Characters:

JAMES PARKER: White male. 50-60 years-old. Slight of build. Bespectacled. Single. Former adjunct English professor.

GINA IANUCELLI: White female. 40-50 years-old. Strong. Real Estate developer. Recently married to JUNE.

JUNE ROBINSON: Black female. 30-40 years-old. Athletic. She is GINA's wife and sole employee; Gina's better half in every way.

JOE DOONAN: White male. Mid 50's. Strong. Married with three children. He is a carpenter and handyman.

Scene:
The living room of a modest but run-down, older house in a medium-size American city.

Time:
Late Spring. The Present.

> Late-morning. The somewhat shabby living room of a
> well-built but modest single-story house. The floor is
> bare. The walls, too, are bare, except for a fireplace with a
> wood surround and mantelpiece in the middle of the stage
> right wall. Upstage of the fireplace is an archway leading
> to a hall and bathroom; downstage of the fireplace is an
> archway leading to the dining room and kitchen beyond.
> The expanse of the upstage wall shows the dingy outlines
> of art that once hung there.
>
> The loud sounds of demolition — power reciprocating saw
> followed by heavy hammering, as with a sledgehammer,

*apparently being produced by only one worker — can
be heard coming from the front porch, just outside the
front door, upstage on the stage left wall. Or, from what
ONCE WAS the front door — for the door itself is off the
hinges and gone. Further downstage on the stage left wall
is a rectangular opening for what ONCE WAS a window
which looks out on the porch.*

*JUNE is seated upon a beat-up couch several feet
downstage of the upstage wall. In front of the couch is an
equally shabby coffee table. These two items, plus a simple
side chair under the window opening on the stage left
wall, are the only pieces of furniture in the room. JUNE is
absorbed in something on her iPad. Lying flat on the floor
in front of the coffee table is JAMES. HE is in a sleeping
bag. Next to him, stage left, is a huge backpack on which
is a hand-lettered sign declaring "OCCUPY." Sounds of
demolition continue for a while, then JAMES sits up.*

JAMES

May I use the toilet? There's still a toilet, right? Water's still on?

JUNE

Oh. Oh. I... Let me... I don't think Gina would... She was pretty
adamant about... I don't know if I should...Um, can you, can you...
hold it?

JAMES

I'm not sure.

The demolition sounds go quiet.

JUNE

Maybe ask her? When she comes back?

JAMES

I don't know if I can wait.

*JOE, the carpenter who has been doing the demolition,
enters the living room through the door opening.*

JOE

Can I use the toilet? It's still in, right?

JUNE

Sure. Through that hall. On the right.

JOE

Thanks.

JOE crosses around in front of JAMES and disappears through the hall.

JUNE

She shouldn't be much longer. She went to that police substation…? Just a few blocks away…?

JAMES

Okay… (*After a slight pause.*) I can't hold it.

JUNE

Oh dear. I don't…

JAMES digs into his backpack and retrieves a plastic jar with a screw top. HE unscrews the lid then brings the open jar into the sleeping bag with him. HE appears to put the jar to his crotch. After half a minute HE pulls the jar, now half-full with yellow liquid, back out from the sleeping bag. The sound of a flushing toilet is heard from the hallway bathroom. JAMES screws the top back on the jar, then places the jar on the coffee table.

JUNE

Oh, that's so disgust—! That makes me so uncomfortable!

JAMES

Sorry. The website says you have to be prepared. Like a Boy Scout.

HE takes a roll of toilet paper out of his backpack and puts it on the coffee table next to the jar.

JUNE

Oh, dear.

JOE enters from the hallway.

JOE

Thank you.

JUNE

You're welcome, Joe. Is there anything else you need?

JOE

No, thank you, missus.

JUNE

Tea? I think, yesterday, Gina brought... The electric is still on. I could make... Do you like Rooibos?

JOE

No, thank you, missus.

JUNE

Water? Ice water? Electric is still on so you can run your tools. The fridge and the other appliances don't go out till this afternoon, with the junk man.

JOE

Thank you, no, missus. I'm fine. Superfine. 600-grit.

JUNE

What...?

JOE

Carpenter's joke. Superfine. Sandpaper...? 600-grit...?

JUNE

Oh! Superfine! I see!

JOE

Yeah.

JUNE

Okay. But if there's anything you need, please let me know.

JOE

I will. Yes. Thank you, missus.
                    (*Indicates JAMES.*)
And, really, I didn't know…

JUNE

No, I understand.

JOE

Thank you, missus.

JOE disappears through the front door opening. JUNE
resumes her work on the iPad. After a while, JAMES speaks:

JAMES

I didn't mean to get him in trouble.

JUNE

He's not in trouble.

JAMES

Good.

JUNE

You are, though.

JAMES

I know.

JUNE

When Gina gets back.

JAMES

I'm thinking positively.

JUNE

I think that's wishful thinking.

JAMES

I'm prepared. "*Be Prepared.*"

JUNE

James, look… I mean… Your option ended a week ago. You know?

                    JAMES

I know.

                    JUNE

You have to accept this.

                    JAMES

I can't.

> *From the porch the loud racket of a reciprocating saw digging deep into wood overpowers the conversation. JAMES covers his ears, groans, scrunches his face in agony, flops back on the floor, then buries his face deep in his sleeping bag.*

                    JUNE

I'm really sorry about this.

> *(Sensing that JAMES didn't hear her, SHE repeats herself, louder.)*

I'M SORRY ABOUT THIS!

> *The demolition noise stops abruptly. JOE peeks in through the window opening:*

                    JOE

Sorry?

                    JUNE

What?

                    JOE

Sorry, I didn't hear you. You want something?

                    JUNE

No, no, nothing, I'm sorry... How is it going?

                    JOE

Pretty good. Railings and balusters are all off and most of the pillars. Last two will be down soon's I get their temporaries secure. Don't want that porch roof comin' down when it shouldn't.

JUNE

Okay.

JOE
(Indicating JAMES in the sleeping bag.)

He givin' you trouble?

JUNE

No. No, he's fine. It's... fine.

JOE

Okay. Just let me know if you need anything.

JUNE

Thank you. I will.

JOE returns to the porch.

JAMES
(Still flat on the floor, his head deep within the sleeping bag.)

He's salvaging?

JUNE

Yes. Gina likes your — the — porch. She wants to use all the pieces on another house.

JAMES

Plus the front door? And all the windows?

JUNE

She'll probably store those.

JAMES

That's all she's saving?

JUNE

I voted for the fireplace mantel and surround, but... she doesn't like them.

JAMES

And she's the boss.

JUNE

Yeah… Listen — James? Listen: You have no standing anymore. I'm begging you, give up on this. Go home.

JAMES sits up.

JAMES

"Home." Haha. Excellent jest.

The demolition sounds resume: intermittent heavy sledgehammer blows.

JUNE

You know what I mean.

JAMES

I know what you mean… She's bringing the police, right?

Hammer blow.

JUNE

That's where she went.

JAMES
(HE digs a notebook out from his backpack.)

I have a plan.

Hammer blow.

JUNE

From that "Occupy" website?

JAMES

Yes.

Hammer blow.

JUNE

That movement — that "Occupy" movement? — it's pretty well past its "sell-by" date, isn't it?

JAMES

Not for me it isn't.

Hammer blow.

JUNE

You're not going to get all radical, all "Off The Pigs" on us, I hope.

JAMES

No. No. I'm not—

Hammer blow.

JUNE

I don't mean to assume that you—

JAMES

I'm not a violent—

Hammer blow.

JUNE

Because I don't really know—

JAMES

If you knew me—

Hammer blow.

JUNE

You've always seemed a decent—

JAMES

I just want—

Hammer blow.

JUNE

But, dealing with police, you know. Sometimes they—

JAMES

No, no. They'll walk away.

(HE waves the notebook.)

It will be fine. No violence… I'm pretty sure…

Several light hammer blows, as one would hammer a nail.

JUNE

Well, I don't think it will exactly be "fine." Not for you.

Two more light hammer blows and one muffled blow, followed by:

JOE

(From the porch.)

Shit! Shit! SHIT! SON of a—! OWWWWW! FUCK ME DEAD! SHIT! PISS! Fuckin' BASTARD!

JUNE leaps to her feet and heads toward the doorway just as JOE bursts into the living room. HE is cursing, alternately holding his hand and shaking it in the air, hopping around blindly:

JOE (cont'd)

God DAMMIT ! — that HURTS!

HE bumps into JUNE.

JOE (cont'd)

Oh, sorry! CRAP! Sorry! Sorry, missus!

JUNE

It's alright. What did you—?

JOE

Goddam THUMB! GodDAMmit!

JUNE

Can I—?

JOE

Ice?

                                    JAMES

Right. Ice.

                                     JOE

You got ice?

                                    JAMES

"RICE." R, I, C, E.

                                    JUNE

Yes.

                                    JAMES

"Rest, Ice, Compression, Elevation."

                                     JOE

Where—?

                                    JUNE

Sit. I'll get it. Sit.

          *JOE, cradling his injury, sits on the sofa. JUNE exits
          through the downstage right archway.*

                                    JAMES

You ought to elevate it. Don't let the blood pool.

          *JOE raises his injured hand above his head. JAMES digs
          into his backpack.*

                                    JAMES

Ow, huh?

                                     JOE

Numb. It's gonna come on again in a minute. Like a sonovabitch.

          *JAMES has retrieved a First Aid manual from his
          backpack, begins to read from it:*

                                    JAMES

"Ice the thumb or finger to reduce pain and swelling… elevate it to
minimize throbbing… don't wrap it…" Huh. "Don't wrap it." I was
wrong there. No compression…

JOE grimaces and begins to bounce his legs to distract himself from the welling pain. JAMES continues to read:

JAMES (cont'd)

"Take an over-the-counter pain reliever... if a blood blister begins under a fingernail, straighten a paper clip, heat the tip in a flame till it is red-hot, touch the red-hot tip to the fingernail and apply slight pressure until the paperclip burns through the—"

JOE

JEEZUS! Pal! Gimme a break!

JAMES

Oh, sure! Sorry!

JUNE returns with ice cubes wrapped in a cloth, hands it to JOE.

JUNE

I hope this is okay. The cubes were all shrunken, so...

JOE

Thanks.

JOE applies the ice pack to his thumb. JAMES is again digging in his backpack.

JUNE

You're so welcome. I'm so sorry! I feel so guilty.

JOE

You don't need to feel—

JUNE

I mean, you're working for me — Gina and me, and...

JOE

It happens. Don't worry about it. Sorry about my... my language back there.

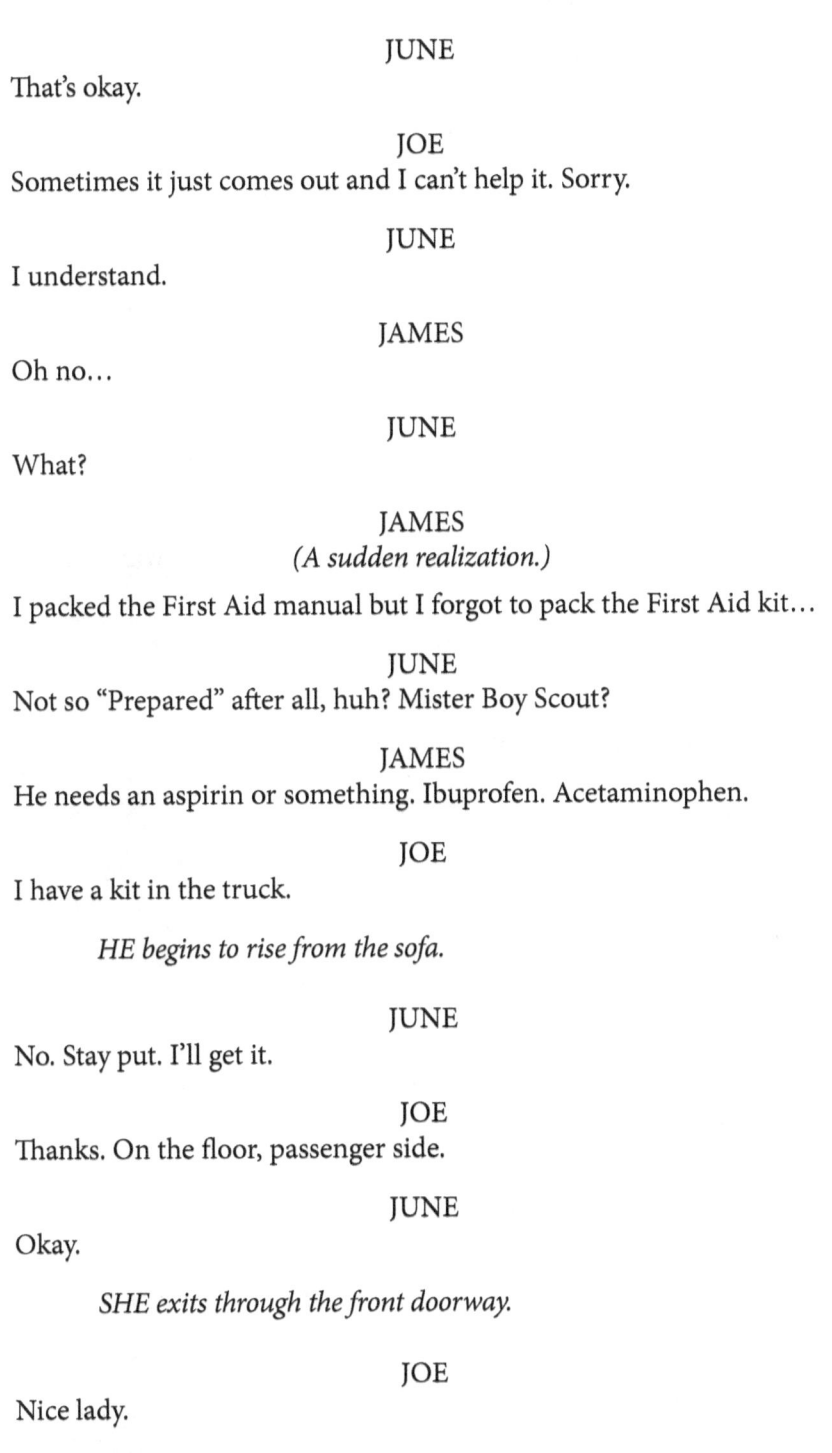

JUNE

That's okay.

JOE

Sometimes it just comes out and I can't help it. Sorry.

JUNE

I understand.

JAMES

Oh no...

JUNE

What?

JAMES
(A sudden realization.)

I packed the First Aid manual but I forgot to pack the First Aid kit...

JUNE

Not so "Prepared" after all, huh? Mister Boy Scout?

JAMES

He needs an aspirin or something. Ibuprofen. Acetaminophen.

JOE

I have a kit in the truck.

HE begins to rise from the sofa.

JUNE

No. Stay put. I'll get it.

JOE

Thanks. On the floor, passenger side.

JUNE

Okay.

SHE exits through the front doorway.

JOE

Nice lady.

                    JAMES
Uh huh.

                    JOE
Gives me a lot of work. Her and her wife.

                    JAMES
Wife…?

                    JOE
The other one there. Gina?

                    JAMES
I didn't realize they were…

                    JOE
Oh, yeah. Few months ago. Had a big deal honeymoon a while back.

                    JAMES
Good. Good for them!

                    JOE
Sure. Everybody has an equal right to be miserable, I always say.

                    JAMES
I…

                    JOE
Right?

                    JAMES
I…

                    JOE
I'm jokin'!

                    JAMES
Yes. Of course. "With Liberty And Justice For All."

                    JOE
She's gettin' the cops, huh?

                    JAMES
Yes… Look, I'm sorry I pulled that trick on you earlier. I've never

done anything like this in my life.

                    JOE
Well, it was a slick move, I'll give ya that.

                    JAMES
It was a chance to get in here. Without breaking and entering.

                    JOE
Yeah.

                    JAMES
I lied to you, as you can see, about coming in here to get the rest of
my furniture, so you'd let me come in.

                    JOE
Yeah, I see.

    JUNE, carrying JOE's First Aid kit, enters.

                    JUNE
They're coming. I saw her car.

                    JAMES
Okay.

                    JUNE
Just down the block.

                    JAMES
Okay.

    *JAMES snuggles deep into his sleeping bag. JOE reaches
    with his good hand for the First Aid kit.*

                    JUNE
I got it.

    *(SHE places the kit on the coffee table, opens it and digs
    through it, looking for the pain medication while SHE
    speaks to JAMES.)*
Get out, James. Leave the furniture for later.

(SHE locates what appears to be a bottle of ibuprofen.)

Then maybe we can work something out. Gina can be flexible. Despite her... outward...

(SHE opens the pill bottle, speaks to JOE.)

You should take two.

(SHE shakes out two pills and hands them to JOE.)

Here. I'll get some water.

JOE

Nah, that's okay.

> *HE takes the pills, pops them in his mouth, crunches them, swallows them.*

JUNE

James?

JAMES

No. I'm not leaving.

JOE
(To JUNE.)

He knows this whole place is comin' down startin' tomorrow, right?

JAMES

I know.

JUNE

He knows.

> *JOE, cradling the ice pack, crosses to JAMES and grabs at him with his good hand, tries to pull JAMES from the floor.*

JOE

Come on, Pal. Don't be crazy.

JUNE

Joe, don't! That's not... That's illegal.

                              JOE

What is? Savin' a guy from havin' a whole house fall on his noggin?

                             JUNE

You can't forcibly evict someone, throw them out, physically. That's why Gina went for the police.

                             JAMES

It will be a case of "He Said, She Said." I'm pretty sure.

         JOE unhands JAMES.

                              JOE

Well, if you want to deal with the cops…

         (HE hands the ice pack to JUNE.)

Thanks, missus. I need to get those last temporaries set up good.

                             JUNE

Are you okay?

                              JOE

Yup. Thanks.

                             JUNE

There's more ice, if you need it again.

                              JOE

Okay.

         HE returns to the work area. JUNE, still holding the ice
         pack, approaches JAMES in his sleeping bag, crouches
         down beside him.

                             JUNE

I don't get it. During this whole process, months and months, we never thought of you as the kind of person who would turn around and do such a nasty thing to us.

                             JAMES

I'm not that kind of person. I'm—

No. You're not. You're a thoughtful, polite, educated person. A reasonable person. So, come on — stand up, meet Gina, meet the police, tell them it's all been cleared up. Okay? Then let's see what we can do. Okay? Okay…?

(SHE stands up.)

Okay, James…? C'mon, stand up… Stand up, James… James! Stand up!

GINA
(From the porch.)

Good morning, Joe.

JOE
(From the porch.)

Mornin', Gina.

JUNE
(Urgent whisper.)

James, for heaven's sake! They're here!

GINA
(From the porch.)

Almost done?

JOE
(From the porch.)

'Nother hour, maybe.

JUNE
(Urgent whisper.)

Please!

GINA
(From the porch.)

Good. Good. Thanks, Joe.

JOE
(From the porch.)

Welcome.

JUNE
(Urgent whisper.)

James!

GINA *enters the living room. Spies JUNE:*

GINA

Is he still…?

(Spies him.)

Ah! James! There you are! Guess what: Good news! No police!

JUNE

Really? No police?

JAMES

No police?

GINA

No police. No one's going to be arrested, no one's going to be cuffed, no one's going to be—(a little laugh.) what do they call it?… Perp-walked? Frog-marched? No. No police. I won't involve them.

JUNE

That's great! James, isn't that great?

JAMES

Yes. Great. Yes.

Two heavy sledgehammer blows are heard from the porch. GINA calls toward the sound:

GINA

Joe?

JOE
(From the porch.)

Gina?

GINA
(Calling.)

Could you grab that stuff from my front seat and bring it in here?

JOE
(From porch.)

Sure.

JUNE

What happened? Did you talk to them?

> *GINA spies the jar on the coffee table, walks toward it while she speaks:*

GINA

The police?

JUNE

Yes.

GINA

As a matter of fact…

> *(Picks up the piss jar.)*

What's this?

JUNE

It's…

JAMES

It's…

JUNE

It's…

JAMES

Pee.

GINA

Pee…?

JAMES

Piss.

GINA

Piss?

JAMES

Urine. Mine.

GINA
(Puts the jar down.)

Gah! It's *warm!*

JAMES

Sorry.

GINA

What the *hell?* How…?

JUNE

He asked to use the toilet, and I thought— I mean, you said…

GINA

I said don't let him move in here, don't let him get comfortable here, but I didn't mean—

(A little laugh.)

Honestly, June! My little Junebug! You always take me so literally!

JUNE

Sorry.

GINA

I'm going to need this table. Could someone… Please…?

(Gestures toward the piss jar.)

JUNE

I'll get it.

JUNE, still holding the ice pack, gingerly grabs the piss jar, looks for someplace to put it, walks to the fireplace and puts it on the mantel. Meanwhile, JOE has entered; HE is carrying a pink box of donuts.

GINA

Donuts, everyone! Joe, where are the coffees?

JOE
(As HE places the box on the coffee table.)

I didn't see no—

GINA

On the floor of the car. Would you mind?

JOE

Sure.

JOE exits. JUNE, still holding the ice pack, walks to the side chair under the stage left window opening and sits. GINA sits on the coffee table near JAMES, opens the donut box and extends it toward JAMES.

GINA

Donut?

JAMES

Ah, no, thank you. Sugar doesn't… I can't…

GINA
(Extending the box toward JUNE.)

June? Got two crüllers here…

JUNE

Gina.

GINA

Hmmmmm? Sweets For The Sweet? Just one…?

JUNE looks away.

                    GINA (cont'd)
Split one with you…?

    JUNE gets up and crosses to GINA.

                    GINA (cont'd)
Come on, it's a special day! Let's celebrate.

    JUNE pulls a cruller from the box, breaks it in half. GINA
    spots the toilet paper roll, unrolls a few sheets, offers them
    to JUNE.

                    GINA (cont'd)
Napkin?

    JUNE accepts the offering. GINA observes the ice pack
    JUNE still holds.

                    GINA (cont'd)
What's that?

                    JUNE
For Joe. Ice. He hurt his thumb.

                    GINA
You're dripping it all over the donuts!

                    JUNE
I'm not "dripping it all over the…" I'll dump it.

    SHE heads toward the dining room/kitchen archway.

                    GINA
Is Joe okay?

                    JUNE
He says he is.

                    GINA
Is he really okay? He doesn't look it.

JUNE

He says he is.

SHE disappears through the archway.

GINA
(A little laugh.)

Don't want to get sued! Not on top of all this other crap going on…

(Again holding the box toward JAMES.)

You sure?

JAMES

Yes. Thank you.

GINA

You are welcome.

SHE sets the box on the coffee table. JOE enters with a small cardboard tray with four cardboard coffee cups.

GINA (cont'd)

Thanks, Joe. Let's see… Joe, I know you like your tea, so I got you a tea, okay? And, James, I don't know about you, so I went ahead and did a black coffee for you, but there's creamer and sugar packs in the bag. Okay?

JUNE enters, half-crüller still in hand.

GINA (cont'd)

Coffee, June. Joe, get your tea. James…?

JAMES removes a coffee from the tray, puts it on the floor beside him. JOE takes his tea container from the tray.

GINA (cont'd)

Joe, take a break. Sit.

SHE gestures toward the chair under the window. JOE crosses toward the chair, sits, while JUNE takes a cup from the tray and crosses to the mantelpiece.

GINA (cont'd)

Joe, you don't have a donut!

JOE

That's okay, I… Okay…

> HE stands. HE seems a little wobbly on his feet, shakes it off,
> steadies himself, then, carrying his unopened tea container,
> crosses to the donut box. HE ponders a moment while the
> OTHERS watch him; favoring his bad thumb HE plucks
> his choice from the box, and, a little embarrassed by the
> attention he has drawn, returns to the chair.

GINA

All right! So! Yes! Celebration! James: you're good! No police!
Serious, serious mess avoided! Victory for you! You're welcome!

JAMES

Thank you.

JUNE

Thank you, Gina.

GINA

So let's enjoy our refreshments, then June and I will — Joe can help,
too, okay, Joe? — we'll get James's stuff out of here. We can toss these
few things into one of our storage units, half-price — right, June? —
at least until he's settled elsewhere and can move it out. Huh? That
good, James? We can work with that?

JAMES

But—

GINA

And we have some vacant apartments. Studios. Decent.

JAMES

Wait—

GINA

Not in this neighborhood of course, but good, solid areas.

                    JAMES

Who said—? I'm— I'm not...

        There is a slight pause...

                    GINA

Not what...?

                    JAMES

Settling. Elsewhere, I mean.

                    GINA

Excuse me?

                    JAMES

This is my home.

                    GINA

James.

                    JAMES

This is my furniture.

                    GINA

This is my house, James. Done. Closed. Stamped, notarized, sealed
and delivered, as of one week ago.

                    JAMES

I don't care.

                    GINA

You don't— Wow. Wow. I don't understand. Have I treated you
unfairly? No. I've gone out of my way to help you. Connected
you with my bankers, gone along with your six month option to
redeem the house, even tried to find you other work. Plus, today,
I've called off a forcible eviction, just so we could take a last stab
at working this out — as reasonable people. Which I thought
you were till now. To my mind you're taking advantage of a nice
person. Me.

                    JAMES

I'm pretty sure there wouldn't have been a forcible eviction today.

GINA

You— Oh, you are, are you?

JAMES

Well, I do believe police won't forcibly evict someone just because they're asked to. Besides, it's "He Said, She Said." I would claim I live here, you would claim I don't. "He Said, She Said." Police wouldn't dare get involved. There's a whole legal process… And you know it.

GINA

Well, well. The professor has done his research.

JAMES

Adjunct—

JOE stands up abruptly.

JOE

I need to get back out there.

GINA

Oh, Joe, Joe… Gee, I'm so sorry you have to be a witness to all of this… But, you bring up a very good point. Just hold on a sec, okay? James, listen to Joe. Joe, tell James why you're here today…

JOE

I— He knows.

GINA

Sure, sure, but just say it again.

JOE

I'm… salvaging the porch. Pillars, railings, balusters…

GINA

Why?

JOE

You want to use them on another house.

GINA

I mean, what's happening to *this* house?

                    JOE

Teardown.

                    GINA

When?

                    JOE

Tomorrow.

                    GINA

What time?

                    JOE

Seven AM... soon's the water and electric are off.

                    GINA

And what would happen to someone who happened to be inside this
house when it is demolished at seven AM?

                    JOE

There wouldn't be no demoli—

                    GINA

No, no, bear with me, Joe — just for argument's sake: what if a
demolition were to take place with someone inside this house? What
would happen to him?

                    JUNE

Gina...

                    GINA
        (Holds up an index finger in JUNE's direction.)

June! — just one sec! Joe...?

        There is a pause...

                    JOE

I don't... He'd... prob'ly be killed.

        A pause...

                    JUNE

Gina, no one is going to—

126

GINA

Well of course not! I'm just saying this machine has started and there's no stopping it. But no harm will come to anyone. And why? James? Why? Because, being naturally compassionate, I would not hesitate to rescue you from this house if you happened to be occupying it when the demolition crew arrives and begins the teardown. Clear?

JAMES

You mean you'll try to eject me. Physically.

GINA

Oh, yes. And legally too, under such a circumstance. June and I. We'd be heroes.

JAMES

If I were in imminent danger.

GINA

Exactly.

JAMES

But, see, I wouldn't be.

GINA

Be what?

JAMES

In imminent danger.

GINA

A house about to come down on your head? That's imminent danger.

JAMES

Yes, but no wrecking crew would begin work knowing the house was occupied. And I will make good and sure they know it's occupied — believe me. So the house would not be coming down on my head. And in that case, any attempt to eject me by force against my will could not in any sense be considered a "rescue," and would expose you to legal liability. And if you should hurt me in any way, I just might have to sue you.

JOE drops his container of tea on the floor.

JOE

Sorry! Ach! Too hot! I lost my— Couldn't switch it to my other— My sore— Sorry! I'll clean—

GINA

No. No. Leave it. What does it matter anyway? Are you sure you're okay?

JUNE

Do you want more ice?

JOE

No. Thank you, missus. I should finish up…

GINA

You sure you can work?

JOE

I'm okay.

> JOE starts toward the front door.

JUNE

Be careful, Joe.

JOE

I will.

GINA

Yes! Please be careful. Leave something standing for the wrecking crew tomorrow! I'm paying them a fortune!

JOE

Okay.

> HE exits, donut in hand. JUNE picks up the fallen coffee container and lid.

GINA

Leave it, June, for heaven's sake. What does it matter?

JUNE

I just…

JAMES

It matters.

> JAMES grabs his backpack and, scootching like an
> inchworm along the floor in his sleeping bag, drags the
> backpack and himself downstage toward JUNE. When HE
> reaches JUNE, HE opens the backpack and extricates a
> roll of paper towels and a plastic trash bag. JAMES takes
> the coffee container and lid from a stunned JUNE, puts the
> trash into the trash bag, then unrolls some sheets of paper
> towel and, still in his sleeping bag, begins to mop up the
> spill. As the paper towels get saturated, HE puts them in
> the trash and unrolls fresh sheets to continue his work.

> A heavy sledgehammer blow is heard from the porch.

GINA
(As JAMES is mopping up.)

It won't matter one whit, come seven o'clock tomorrow morning, you know…

JAMES

It matters to me.

GINA

June, is this crazy, or what?

> Hammer blow.

> JUNE stoops to the floor, unrolls sheets of paper towel and
> begins to help JAMES mop up the spill.

GINA (cont'd)

Are you—? What are you doing?!

JUNE

Helping. Obviously…

> Hammer blow.

> JUNE and JAMES continue their work for a bit in silence.

Hammer blow.

Hammer blow.

GINA
Oh, for the love of—!

Hammer blow.

GINA (cont'd)
You know you're cleaning a floor that won't even exist twenty-four hours from now, don't you? Huh? Little Junebug…?

Hammer blow.

JUNE
I know…

Hammer blow.

Hammer blow.

GINA
You're as crazy as he is… I can't believe it. He brought trash bags?! And paper towels?!

(*SHE pulls a cigarette from a pack, lights it as SHE speaks.*)

I mean, this is crazy…

The floor is clean to JAMES's satisfaction. HE cinches close the trash bag, puts it aside.

Hammer blow.

GINA (cont'd)
(*Blowing smoke.*)

This whole day…

Hammer blow.

GINA (cont'd)

Crazy…

JAMES

Please don't smoke in my house.

GINA

This is not—!

A brief pause, then GINA deliberately drops the cigarette and grinds it into the floor.

GINA (cont'd)

There. Satisfied…?

ALL THREE stare at the burned spot on the floor. Then JUNE retrieves the trash bag, picks up the dead cigarette and throws it in with the rest of the trash. As JUNE is cinching up the bag, GINA grabs her by the waist and pulls JUNE to herself.

GINA (cont'd)

Well, I don't know, dear, but I sense we're at an impasse here. I think it might be time to place that call. Whaddya think?

JUNE

What call?

GINA

To the scary law firm? You know: Johnson, Weiner, Cox, Peters, and O'Toole?

(SHE gives JUNE a little squeeze.)

Huh? Whaddya say?

(JUNE doesn't respond.)

Or the other one? — Makem, Hurt, Goode and Hart…? Huh…? Or maybe Pierce, Dice and Frye…?

JUNE

James… We… we don't mean to make fun.

GINA

(Releases JUNE from her grasp.)

No, we don't. Oh, no, we don't! We're definitely not making fun. In fact we're dead serious. In fact we retain the best lawyers in this whole damn county, and we will not hesitate to ask them to make life very, very difficult for you, if necessary.

JAMES

I will deal with it.

GINA

Oh-ho, and you will be dealt with, believe you me!

JAMES

(HE has scrupulously done his research.)

Yes. Your scary law firm will file an unlawful detainer suit with the county. But first you must give me five days' notice of your intention to file. Then after the filing, the matter will be reviewed by a judge. That will definitely take some time. And if the judge decides you have a case, it will go to the Sheriff. So, filing-to-judge-to-Sheriff? That's a good thirty days or so. And, are you giving me your five days' notice right now? That would bring us a good thirty-five days out. A lot can happen in thirty-five days.

> *JOE enters through the front doorway. HE is holding a pizza box and a bottled water.*

JOE

Missus? Gina?

> *GINA wheels on JOE*

GINA

WHAT?!

JOE

I'm sorry, I think he— I think James, here, ordered a pizza? The guy says it's paid for already?

JAMES

Yes, it's mine. Thank you, Joe.

JOE approaches JAMES with the pizza box. Just as JOE is about to lower the box to JAMES, HE hesitates. Speaks to GINA:

JOE

Is it… okay?

GINA

Of course it's okay! I'm not his jailer!

JOE hands the pizza box and the water bottle to JAMES.

GINA (cont'd)

Jeepers, Joe. What do you think of me, anyway?

JOE

Not much.

GINA

What?

JOE

I mean, I, I, I don't.

GINA

You don't…?

JAMES has opened the box of pizza and has begun to eat a slice.

JOE

I mean, I think of you, sure, but I don't have bad thoughts.

GINA

Bad thoughts?

JOE

I mean… I mean… I don't mean thoughts that are, are, you know, impure, or anything. I mean they're not bad thoughts. You know? I mean, like, my thoughts aren't like you're bad, or anything. I mean—

GINA

No, no, I know, I know! Alright… Don't… Let's just… drop the—

JOE

Alright.

GINA

Alright… Joe, those… those things, those… thingies? Out there?
Those, those—

JOE

Temporaries?

GINA

Yes, those. Are they—? Are you done?

JOE

One more to go. Then I can get the last pillar out. My thumb's slowin'
me down a little bit, but…

GINA

June, get him more ice, will you?

(JUNE exits through the archway.)

Sit down, Joe.

JOE

I gotta get—

GINA

Sit down! You're going to ice that thumb!

JAMES
(Still eating pizza.)

"Twenty minutes on, twenty minutes off."

JOE sits on the chair under the window opening. HE
lowers his head between his knees.

GINA

You're a liability to me, you know, working in that condition.

JOE

I'm okay.

GINA

Not from the looks of you. You're feeling woozy, aren't you? And your thumb is all purple.

JOE

I've had worse.

JUNE enters with the ice pack.

GINA

Well, I don't want you to have worse today…

(JUNE gives the ice pack to JOE who applies it to his thumb.)

…of all days… Thank you, June…
(To JOE.)

You go and knock that porch roof down on yourself because you can't handle your tools correctly, and all of a sudden I've got ten times the trouble I have already.

JOE
(To JUNE.)

Thank you, missus.

JUNE

You're welcome.

JUNE walks up to the sofa, sits. GINA wheels on JAMES.

GINA

And what am I going to do about YOU?!

JAMES
(Still eating.)

Let me keep my home.

GINA

This is not your— That was a rhetorical question. Shouldn't an English teacher recognize a rhetorical question when he hears one?

JAMES
(Correcting her.)

Adjunct lecturer in English.

GINA

Adjunct, part-timer, whatever… Teacher… What is it they say?
"Those who can, do; those who can't, teach"? Is that it?

JAMES

I believe so.

GINA

Okay, teacher, here's a real, non-rhetorical question for you: When
that pizza's gone, how will you eat after today, if you don't get out of
that sleeping bag and get the hell out of my house? Hmm? You going
on some thirty-five day hunger strike or something? Because we're
not going to feed you. You can count on that.

JAMES

Actually, I have arranged for a pizza and bottles of water to arrive
here every day for some time to come.

GINA

My god. You're kidding me.

JUNE

What was that idea we discussed this morning, Gina? You know…

GINA

Putting him in an apartment.

JAMES

No!

GINA

No. No! Listen to me! I'm TALKING! And if you don't want to hear
what I have to say you'll have to either stop up your ears or get up and
leave the building…

(JAMES is silent.)

Alright… Now, June is quite sympathetic to your situation. She's
empathetic. That's a good adjective, hmm? English Teacher?

Empathetic? Anyway, June used to be a teacher's aide, you know, and she reminds me that education cutbacks have been brutal. Well, I know this. I'm a business person, I read the news. I keep up. "Last Hired, First Fired." Right? I get it…

(SHE comes to rest at the fireplace, putting an elbow on the mantel, just inches from the piss jar.)

And you've lost half your teaching positions.

                    JUNE

Three-quarters

                    GINA

Through no fault of— What? Three—?

                    JAMES

Three of my four adjunct positions.

                    GINA

Three out of four…

(SHE absent-mindedly picks up the piss jar, examines it as SHE speaks.)

Well, that's even —

(Suddenly realizes.)

GAH!

(Slams the jar back down on the mantel.)

June! I thought I— James! This is disgusting! Go dump this in the toilet! For heaven's sake!

JAMES instinctively begins to rise in obedience but instantly stops himself, resumes his position on the floor.

                    JAMES

No. No. I prefer not to.

                    GINA

Jee-zus. June…?

JUNE

Why should I?

JOE
(Rising from the chair.)

I'll do it.

GINA

Would you? Oh, thank you, Joe. Thank you! You're a hero!

> *JOE steadies himself, and cradling his ice-packed thumb, HE crosses to the fireplace, retrieves the piss jar, crosses to the hall/bathroom archway.*

GINA (cont'd)
(Calling after him.)

A Prince, Joe! You're the best!

> *JOE hesitates, stops at the archway, fumbles with the jar lid.*

JOE

Um… I can't… My thumb… I can't… open the lid.

GINA

Oh, for the love of—! Well, I'm not opening it!

JAMES

Hand it to me, Joe…

> *JOE crosses to JAMES, who opens the piss jar and hands it back to JOE. JOE, a little unsteady on his feet, carries it past GINA, who shrinks from the loathed object.*

GINA

Ick. Ick, ick, ICK!

JOE

Sorry.

> *JOE exits.*

And I resigned from my fourth…

There is a slight pause

GINA

You…? What?

JUNE

James!

GINA

Resigned?

JUNE

Oh, James.

GINA

You purposely quit?

JAMES

Yes.

JUNE

Why, James?

JAMES

To do this, for as long as I need to.

GINA

Do this *what*?

JAMES

Occupy my house.

GINA

This is not your—!

(Heaves a great sigh.)

Oh, June… I'm just exhausted. Would you mind, Honey? You know how I hate to talk about anything that costs us money, especially handouts to the… to the homeless. Would you tell the… the *current occupant* here… what we were talking about? I'm just pooped all of a sudden.

SHE sits on the sofa.

> JUNE

We want to help you get re-established, James, and I think I have a possible solution…

> *(The sound of a flushing toilet is heard from the hallway.)*

It involves an apartment building I bought—

> GINA

With my help.

> JUNE

With… yes, with Gina's generous help… I bought a small, four-unit building. We just fixed up all the units and they're ready for occupancy. I was thinking, maybe I could let you use one of them—

> GINA

Short-term, June. Don't give away the store. Three months, six months, I don't know…

JOE enters, carrying the empty jar.

> JOE
> *(To GINA:)*

Excuse me, I'm sorry, what do you want me to do with…? Does he want…?

> *(To JAMES, about the jar.)*

Do you want this back, or…?

> JAMES

Yes. Thank you.

JAMES takes the jar from JOE, puts it in his backpack.

> JOE
> *(Crouches down to JAMES's level.)*

You're welcome… and it's none of my business, but, I overheard… Look, take the deal. June got a real decent place there. I've worked in all the units. They're solid. And June and Gina? They're tops around here. Everybody knows it. People have a problem, Gina's on the phone to me right away and it's fixed. Plumbing guys love to work for them. Electricians. These two have the fairest rents in the area. Ask the rental agents. You can't go wrong. None of my business, but, take the deal.

JAMES

Do those units have fireplaces?

JOE

N-n-no...

GINA

No. They don't have fireplaces.

JAMES

Porches?

JUNE

No.

JOE

No.

JAMES

And the rent would be...?

JUNE
(Glances at GINA.)

I think... We've been saying that... I think we've pretty much decided that I could... waive the rent. For a few months. So you can get back on your feet.

JOE

Sounds like a pretty sweet deal.

GINA

"Sweet deal?" It's free money!

JAMES

Is there a balcony?

                              GINA

No! There's no balcony!

                              JOE

No balcony.

                             JAMES

I'd at least like some sort of outdoor space.
                    (Takes a bite of pizza.)

                              JOE

I'm sorry, I just thought—

          *(Stands up abruptly, pulls the ice pack from his thumb,
          hands it to JUNE.)*

Okay, I gotta get back to work.

                             JUNE

Be careful.

          JOE exits the living room, back to his work on the porch.

                              GINA

Fireplaces? Porches? Balcony? These are apartments, basic
apartments. What did you think?

                             JAMES

I can't give up everything I have here in my own home.

                             JUNE

James—

                              GINA

Are you delusional?

                             JUNE

Gina—

                              GINA

This is not your home! You defaulted on your mortgage a year ago, I
bought this house at Sheriff's auction six months ago, and your right
to redeem expired last week. You failed to buy it back. *You failed!* This

is my house and you are trespassing on private property.

                              JAMES
I am not trespassing, I am protesting. I am exercising my first
amendment right to free speech. I'm staging a sit-in…

        (HE pulls out his notebook from the backpack, flips to a
        page, reads.)
"…to protest the Fraud and Corruption of the Rigged System that
killed the Middle Class and robbed me of my Employment, my
House, and my Human Dignity."

                              GINA
What kind of protest is it when nobody even knows you're doing it,
except me and June? And Joe.

                              JAMES
People will know. Eventually. Word will get out.

                              GINA
Why don't you just take it outside, then? Huh? Take it to the sidewalk.

                              JAMES
And leave my house to you and the demolition crew…? Besides, on
the sidewalk you'd have me arrested for blocking a public right-of-
way. No, I'm staying right here. Legally. I didn't break and enter. The
door was open this morning — well, there was no door! I admit I
manipulated Joe, so I'm guilty of lying, yes, but I'm not a trespasser.
I'm a Constitutionally Protected Protester. I will eat here, I will sleep
here, I will work here… I guess I'm a squatter. In my own home. I'm a
re-squatter.

                              GINA
You'll "work" here? What "work?"

                              JAMES
My poetry.

                              GINA
Your poetry. How much does that pay?

JUNE

What do you want, James? Be specific. Please help us understand.

GINA

Yes. Do you have "demands?" Don't extortionists generally have "demands?"

JAMES

If you put it that way — Justice. I demand Justice.

The sound of a heavy sledgehammer blow from the porch.

GINA

No such thing. You must have learned that by now.

Heavy hammer blow.

JAMES

And six more months to buy my house back.

GINA

Here we go again! No. No! It's over. No!

Two heavy hammer blows.

JUNE

But, you'd owe six more months interest on top of the re-purchase price; plus the previous six months interest, and all the legal fees, past and future. And you don't even have a job!

GINA

There's no Justice, James; it's sad, and I'm sorry about that. Truly sorry, which you may or may not understand. However, there is the Law. And the Law says all your options have expired. And the Law is the Law.

Several lighter hammer blows, as when one hammers a nail.

GINA
(*About the noise.*)

Gah! I cannot hear myself think!

144

JUNE calls out the window.

JUNE

Joe?

Several more hammer blows.

JUNE (cont'd)

Joe?! Could you please— Joe, here, take this ice and take a short— Joe, why don't you take an early lunch break and keep that thumb iced? Okay? Gina's worried about you. And I am, too; the way you're—

JOE
(From the porch.)

I'm okay.

JUNE

No. We insist. You'll have plenty of time to finish after lunch.

JOE
(From the porch.)

Okay.

JUNE hands the ice pack through the window to JOE.

JOE
(From the porch.)

Thanks.

JUNE

Welcome.

(To JAMES.)

You didn't hear the rest of my proposal. Okay...? Now, in exchange for the rent, you caretake. Okay?

JAMES

Caretake.

JUNE

Simple chores. You manage a few light tasks around the building. Make sure the stairwells are clean. Keep the dumpster areas clear. Like that. Field calls from the other tenants. You know. Be kind of a go-between for us, take care of other things we might need occasionally. Part-time. Just till you get back on your feet. The place is really nice—

GINA

Semi-furnished studio. Top floor. Clean. Full kitchen. Full bath. June did a nice job. She can draw up the papers and you can have the key this afternoon.

JUNE

You'll have a nice place to stay right away, rent-free, for a while, and we all stay friendly... What do you think...?

There is a slight pause...

JAMES

When did you buy the building?

JUNE

Ahh, I closed on it, ahhh... When was that, Gina? Just before the wedding, right?

GINA

Yeah. Crazy time.

JUNE

Right. Six months ago. The same week Gina bought your— this place.

JAMES

Auction?

JUNE

Yes.

JAMES

Foreclosure?

GINA

Of course.

JAMES

I'd hate to take advantage of somebody else's misfortune. Even indirectly.

GINA

Oh, what? June is the *direct* advantage-taker? The *direct* oppressor?

JAMES

Well, in a way, yes.

GINA

Let me make this very clear to you. We are offering this proposal — which will not remain on the table much longer, right, June? — in lieu of all-out legal action. I mean the full weight of civil court. The Law. And right now, despite what you may think, The Law, and Time, Sir, are not your very best friends. Sit-in? You won't have half an ass left to sit on! I mean, Jeezus! Have you always been such a stubborn little prick or are you just trying it on for size?

JUNE stands up abruptly.

JUNE

Okay, Gina...

(*SHE takes GINA by the elbow. To JAMES.*)

Sorry. We'll be right back.

GINA breaks away from JUNE.

GINA

No! No! I want him to explain! Please! Explain yourself! What Justice? What Injustice? Explain, dammit! In simple words and phrases, please, Professor, so the little ten-percent of my brain that I use can understand you.

JUNE

Gina!

JUNE again takes GINA by the elbow guides her toward the upstage archway and THEY exit. A brief silence. JAMES remains sitting upright on the floor. An offstage argument between GINA and JUNE begins, their voices rising and falling.

GINA
(Offstage.).

… am not!…

JUNE
(Offstage.)

… again and again!…

> *As the offstage argument progresses, the LIGHTS change, the SOUND of rumbling thunder is heard, followed by the SOUND of rain on the roof which grows in intensity. Soon the walls of the living room brighten, and we perceive paintings hung on the walls, full bookshelves on the walls, a wall clock, etcetera, even a gorgeous oriental rug on the floor — objects that make a house a home. (See Production Notes at end of play.*)*

> *JAMES begins a sequence of silent actions, oblivious to the rancor beyond the living room. JUNE and GINA's offstage argument continues throughout the pantomime:*

> *JAMES slithers out of his sleeping bag.*

> *HE stands up straight.*

> *HE stretches.*

GINA
(Offstage.)

… makes me crazy!…

> *HE crosses to the window opening on the stage left wall.*

> *HE pantomimes raising a sash.*

> *HE takes a deep breath of air — HE can smell the rain!*

JUNE
(Offstage.)

… always resort to bullying!…

    HE lowers the sash.

GINA
(Offstage.)

… have my limit!…

    HE shivers just a little bit. HE crosses to the stage right
    fireplace, crouches.

JUNE
(Offstage.)

… like they're inferior!…

    HE pantomimes lighting a match. HE holds the "match" to
    the "wood" in the fireplace. HE blows out the match.

GINA
(Offstage.)

… "fireplaces?!"…

    The LIGHTS change; the glowing "fire" is warming the
    room, making it cozy.

    JAMES warms his hands before the blazing fire, loves how
    it feels, stands, turns, feels the warmth on his back.

JUNE
(Offstage.)

… don't even realize it!…

    HE hears a "knock" on the door.

    HE crosses up to the door, "opens" it.

HE is thrilled to greet his "visitor." HE takes his "visitor's" raincoat, shakes off the drops of rain, ushers his visitor to the chair below the window opening, "conversing" animatedly.

GINA
(Offstage.)

… *"porches?!"…*

HE crosses up to the coffee table, mimes pouring a cup of tea. Conversing. HE crosses to the chair, hands the tea and saucer to his guest. Conversing.

JUNE
(Offstage.)

… *embarrass yourself…*

HE crosses back up to the coffee table. Still conversing. HE pours himself a cup of tea, drops two cubes of sugar into it. Conversing. HE crosses with his tea to the mantel of the fireplace, lounges there, crossing his legs elegantly, as one does when lounging against one's own mantelpiece.

GINA
(Offstage.)

… *"balconies?!"…*

HE converses animatedly with his guest, laughing often (silently, of course), sipping his tea. Oh, no! — his guest must be on his way! HE crosses to the chair, relieves his guest of his teacup.

GINA
(Offstage.)

… *unlike you…*

HE ushers his guest up toward the door. HE retrieves his guest's raincoat, helps him on with it, shakes his guest's hand. HE opens the door and lets his guest out, waves to him a few times.

JUNE
(Offstage.)

… more flies with honey…

HE stands staring out the door for a bit, waves one more time. It's cold and wet outside. HE shuts the door. HE crosses down to his sleeping bag.

GINA
(Offstage.)

… run all over you!…

HE slides into his sleeping bag.

HE sits silently. The LIGHTS begin to change; the SOUNDS of the "rainstorm" begin to fade away; the "fire" slowly dies; the paintings, bookshelves, carpeting, etcetera are disappearing…

JUNE
(Offstage.)

… sometimes I don't even recognize you.

GINA
(Offstage.)

Don't say that, Honey. Oh, don't say that…

LIGHTS finally resume original settings; JAMES, in his sleeping bag, sits in silence for a few beats, then JOE peeks in through the stage left window opening, calls to JAMES:

JOE

Hey… James…?

JAMES

Joe…?

JOE

Where are—? Are they…?

JAMES

Back in the bedroom I think.

JOE

I need to tell her— Gina— I need to tell her I can't… I'm kind of all in
bits here… With my thumb…

JAMES

It's bad?

JOE

Real bad. Feels like it's gonna pop. I think I should go to the
Emergency.

JAMES

Then you should go.

JOE

She'll kill me. I need to finish this job. But I know I'll be forever at the
Emergency.

JAMES

What's left to do?

JOE

Get the last pillar out. I got the four-by-four temporary up next to it
but I gotta clinch-nail it then cut out the pillar and take it down. Also,
I feel a little… Hey, could you take a peek in that first-aid kit behind
you there?

JAMES

Sure…

*JAMES finds JOE's kit that was left on the coffee table,
opens the kit.*

JOE

That bottle of ibo… ibu… iboproof… pain-killers, there? Not the
CVS twelve-hour bottle, the other one…?

JAMES

Yeah?

JOE

Those pills have a number stamped on 'em?

JAMES opens the bottle, shakes out a pill, examines it.

JAMES

Yeah.

JOE

I knew it. They're my muscle-relaxers. I keep 'em in that old ibu —
that old bottle — in case my back spasms, like it does sometimes.
I usually only take one, but I ate two of 'em this morning. Heh-
heh — oh boy… And with my damn thumb feeling like it's big as a
watermelon, I can hardly hold my Sawzall.

JAMES

Oh boy… Maybe she could help? Or June, maybe?

JOE

I don't know… those pillars weigh a ton. They used different woods
way back when they built this place. Southern Pine. Not like this
second-growth Doug Fir shit nowadays.

*JAMES replaces the first-aid kit on the coffee table, briefly
glances over his shoulder toward the hall archway behind
him, turns back to JOE:*

JAMES

Any other time, I'd help. But…

JOE

Yeah. It's alright. I get it. I'll just…

JAMES

Again, I'm sorry I deceived you like that. I like you and I'm sorry I got
you in the middle of all of my mess.

JOE

It's okay. I gotta do my job out here, but, I get what you're doing.

JAMES

You do?

                              JOE
Yeah. Union Strong!… You Union?

                             JAMES
Not any more…

                              JOE
Yeah. Me neither…

                             JAMES
Okay.

                              JOE
Okay…

          There is a slight pause…

                             JAMES
There's always… the paper clip.

                              JOE
Paper clip?

                             JAMES
That you heat? For your thumb? And push…?

                              JOE
Oh. Crap…

                             JAMES
Yeah…

                              JOE
Yeah… Well, it's worth a try, I guess.

                             JAMES
They'd probably do something similar at the Emergency Room.

                              JOE
Yeah… You got one?

                             JAMES
No.

JOE

Crap.

> GINA and JUNE enter from the upstage hallway. GINA
> speaks to JAMES as SHE enters:

GINA

I'm sorry… James…? I'm sorry. Okay?

JAMES

Okay.

GINA

I'm sorry if you were offended. Okay?

JAMES

Okay.

> GINA spots JOE.

GINA

Joe. How are you doing? That ice working okay?

JOE

Well…

JAMES

He needs a paper clip.

GINA

A paper clip?

JAMES

For his thumb.

GINA

For his thumb?

JAMES

To relieve the pressure.

JUNE

I might have one.

*SHE digs in her bag, finds some papers held together with
a paper clip, removes it, holds it up.*

JUNE

This okay?

JAMES

I think so. And a match. Or a lighter.

JUNE

Gina…?

GINA

What do you need a lighter for?

JAMES

You heat the paper clip till it's red hot then you press the tip into the
nail till it burns through and allows the built-up blood to escape. It
relieves the pressure. And the pain.

GINA

That sounds awful.

JAMES

It's in the first-aid manual.

JUNE

Joe, maybe you should quit for now and get over to the Emergency
Room. Or an Urgent Care.

JOE

Well…

GINA

He'd be there all day. Joe, are you okay with this, this, paper clip…
thing?

JOE

Sure.

GINA

Well, come in here and let's get it over with. Let's get this whole day
over with, for heaven's sake…

JOE enters through the doorway. The muscle-relaxants
HE's taken have clearly compromised his motor functions.

GINA (cont'd)

Come. Sit on the sofa. Here's my lighter.

JOE carefully sits, takes GINA's lighter.

JOE

Damn! — Will ya look at this! An old Ronson! That's... fuckin'
awesome!

HE fumbles with the flip-cover a bit, then tries a few
times, unsuccessfully, to operate the lighter.

JUNE

He can't— I'll do it.

JOE

Thank you, Missus...

JOE hands the lighter to JUNE.

JOE (cont'd)

Ronson lighters... Makes me wish I still smoked... Camels...
Luckies... "L.S.M.F.T..."

JUNE sits beside JOE and pulls JOE's hand to her lap,
unravels some toilet paper off the roll on the coffee table
and packs a wad of toilet paper around JOE's thumb.

JOE (cont'd)

"Lucky Strike Means Fine Fuckin' Tobacco..."

GINA

So, James. Let me start fresh here...

JUNE straightens the paper clip, lights the lighter and
holds the paper clip tip over the flame.

GINA (cont'd)

Now, June, as you probably have noticed by now, is a much better person than I am. No, I'm serious! June tunes in where I tune out; June sees where I am blind; and June hears where I am deaf. June is, in every sense, my better half. So: June tells me I should make more of an effort to hear you.

JUNE extinguishes the lighter then gingerly applies the red-hot paper clip tip to JOE's thumbnail.

GINA (cont'd)

I admit, I go to a pretty jaded place when someone throws that word at me: "Justice." "Injustice."

JUNE pulls the paper clip away from JOE's thumbnail.

JUNE

Oh, god, Joe! I don't know if—

JOE

It'll feel much better, I can tell. Go ahead and press. Put the metal to the... Put the petal to... Push that fucker right in there.

GINA

Do it, June. He'll be fine.

JOE

I'll be fine. Superfine. 600-grit. I'll just be... lookin' down from... up here...

JUNE

Okay... It's cooled off too much...

JUNE relights the lighter and holds the paper clip over the flame.

GINA
(To JAMES.)

I have a personal relationship with "Injustice." We go way back together. Been in bed together. You know what I mean? June, too. Right, June?

JUNE
(Concentrating on her work.)

Mm hmm…

GINA

So I should have been more sensitive to you.

JUNE again extinguishes the lighter and applies the red-hot tip of the paper clip to JOE's thumbnail.

GINA (cont'd)

So: "Justice," James. What exactly do you mean by that?

JOE

Press. Hard. I can't feel nothin'.

JUNE

Okay…

GINA

Hmm? Convince me I should give you another six months. Convince me that — when every legal option has been explored and exhausted but you haven't liked the way it turned out and you just wish everything could be different — convince me that you haven't gotten "Justice." I'm listening. Please. Enlighten me.

Suddenly a great gout of blood spurts from JOE's thumb and spatters all over GINA, who has been standing nearby.

GINA (cont'd)

Oh! SHIT! June!

JUNE

Sorry. Sorry, Joe…

JOE

No problémo…

JUNE urgently wraps the toilet paper wad around JOE's thumb to absorb the freely-flowing blood. GINA grabs the toilet paper roll, pulls off sheets of tissue and dabs frantically at the blood splattered on her.

GINA

Jeezus! Does he have AIDS? I hope he doesn't have AIDS. Are you
HIV, Joe?

JUNE

He doesn't have AIDS, Gina! Calm down! Joe, are you alright?

JOE

Yeah. It felt better right away.

JUNE

You sure?

JOE

Yeah. I feel great! Thank you.

JUNE

We should probably bandage it.

JOE

I have some in the first-aid…

  HE stands up from the sofa and immediately sits again.
Whoa…

JUNE

You okay?

JOE

Yeah…

  HE stands up from the sofa again and immediately sits
  back down again.

JUNE

Lie back, Joe. You look pale.

JOE

…all in bits here…

GINA

Joe — shit — Joe, lie down. June, help him.

JUNE helps JOE stretch out on the sofa, opens the first-aid kit, tends to JOE's thumb as she speaks.

JUNE

Just stretch out here for now, Joe. Rest for a bit. You'll be fine.

JOE

I'll be Superfine. Ultrafine. 800-grit. 3M, wet-or-dry…

JUNE

Let's get a bandage on there. It's not bleeding much, but you don't want it to get dirty.

GINA

Ach! I'm a mess! Dammit!

GINA hurries toward the upstage hall/bathroom archway; exits. JUNE finishes up with JOE, carefully dabs toilet tissue at herself, at JOE, anyplace else blood may have spattered, as SHE speaks:

JUNE

Joe…?

JOE

Hello?

JUNE

You aren't… HIV positive, are you…?

JOE

I'm AB.

JUNE

A… B?

JOE

My blood type?

JUNE

No, No. HIV positive. It's a—

                                JOE

I'm AB, I'm pretty sure...

                                JUNE

Okay...

                                JAMES

He'd probably know, if he...

                                JUNE

Right... Of course...

            JUNE ministers to JOE's wound as SHE speaks to JAMES.

                            JUNE (cont'd)
Gina... when she was in her twenties? — You don't know this
about her. Joe does. — Gina... she was evicted from two different
apartments by two different landlords. Her... sexual orientation...
was *reported* to them. Two evictions. One after the other. No law
against it. Not in this state, anyway, back then. And no federal law, of
course. Absolutely nothing she could do.

                                JAMES

Right.

                                JUNE
She stayed with friends — no help from her parents — and she
worked so hard... saved till she could buy her own apartment
building. Six units. She moved into one and rented the others to
anyone with decent credit, no other questions asked. I was her second
tenant. She welcomed me. Respected me. Understood me. And I
loved her for that.

                                JAMES

Of course.

                                JUNE
For that, and for many other things... To a lot of people, including
me, she's kind of a hero. But not to you. I think you just don't like her.

                                JAMES
It's... No, it's not personal... It's the principle.

JUNE

This isn't just revenge? Some way to get back at Gina, for taking the house?

JAMES

No... it's not her.

GINA

(From upstage. Has overheard.)

Oh, come on, it's me alright. It's me: Gina The Hero. Here I come to save the day.

JUNE

Are you okay, Gina?

GINA

I'm fine.

JOE

Superfine! 800-grit... Super... hero... fine...

GINA

What—?

JUNE

It's a... a carpenter's joke. Sandpaper, something. Grade...? I don't know.

JOE

Ultrafine...

GINA

Joe, just... just feel better, okay? I need you to finish up out there.

JOE

Sure thing.

GINA crosses to JAMES..

GINA

Bullshit, James. Bullshit. Not personal? Principle? Sorry, but you can't stand on principle here without standing on me. So *I* am taking this *very* personally. You know how this is going to end, don't you? All

163

that research, all the case law you've read up on—? Tells you just one story, right? Spoiler Alert: you lose in the end.

There is a pause. JAMES is silent.

GINA (cont'd)

Mm hmm... So...

(With sudden, urgent passion.)

You're hurting me, James. And I don't understand why. If it's really not personal — which is hard to believe, because, I admit, I can... trigger — then why? Why are you doing this to me?

JAMES

Because... Because I...

(A little choked up, emotional...)

I love my little house.

GINA
(Literally rolls her eyes.)

Oh, boy...

JAMES wipes at his eyes, then rummages in his backpack and pulls out a notebook, flips it open, finds a page, reads:

JAMES

Homeless, Homesick,
Homebody, Home Alone;
Home cooking, Home run,
Make yourself at home.
Home is where the heart is,
Home Sweet Home.
Anywhere I hang my hat,
A House Is Not A Home.
Homeowner, Homewrecker,
Homeland, Homeward Bound,
Won't You Come Home, Bill Bailey?
Can't go home again.
It takes a heap of living.

Home, Home On The Range,
Back Home Again In Indiana.
Sweet Home, Alabama,
There's no place like home.
Daddy's Home, Home free,
Home For The Holidays.
Homing in,
Honey, I'm home.
It ain't much,
But it's home.

(He has finished reading the poem.)

GINA

What the hell…?

JAMES turns a page, reads:

JAMES

She waits for me
Tho' I do roam;
Waits, content,
Tho' all alone.
Till when, at last,
On path of stone,
I come to her.
I'm here.
I'm home.

(He has finished reading the poem.)

GINA

This is, what? Your Hallmark poetry?

JAMES turns a few other pages, finds the right one, clears his throat, reads:

JAMES

Stay, stay at home, my heart, and rest;
Home-keeping hearts are happiest,
For those that wander they know not where

Are full of trouble and full of care;
To stay at home is best
Then stay at home, my heart, and rest;
The bird is safest in its nest;
O'er all that flutter their wings and fly
A hawk is hovering in the sky;
To stay at home is best.

(He has finished reading the poem.)

Silence... then:

GINA

You get paid for that? Greeting cards, or...?

JOE
(From his prone position on the sofa.)

Those are nice.

JAMES

Oh, thanks, Joe.

JOE

Especially that last one there.

JAMES

Actually, that one? That's not mine.

JOE

Oh.

JAMES

It's Longfellow... Henry Wadsworth...?

JOE

Oh. Well, that first one there?

JAMES

Mm hmm?

JOE

That's yours?

JAMES

Yes; that and the other one.

JOE

You repeat "Home" a lot in that one. "Home" this, "Home" that. "Home, Home, Home." Lotsa "Homes" in there…

JAMES

Yes, well, that's kind of the point, actually. It's a montage of—

GINA

What is this, some adult education poetry workshop or something? Poets Anonymous? Joe, are you feeling better?

JOE

Ummm…

HE swings his legs to the floor and stands, sways.

Whew… Boy, I don't—

JUNE takes hold of his elbow, guides him.

JUNE

Lie on the floor with your feet up on the coffee table. Come on. Here, next to James.

SHE pushes JAMES's backpack aside and assists JOE to lie flat on the floor, stage left of JAMES. JOE's head is downstage and his feet are up on the coffee table.

JUNE (cont'd)

James, keep your eye on him. I don't like how pale he looks.

JOE

Whew… I don't usually… Sorry, Gina…

JUNE

It's all right. Just take it easy.

JAMES

Don't worry about it.

GINA

Oh, yeah, that's right, don't worry about it. It's all right. Everything will be fine. Ultrafine. The Universe will take care of everything.

JUNE

Gina.

GINA

Well, I mean, come on, this is just a great little situation, isn't it? A poetry-spouting squatter and a defective handyman side-by-side on the floor of a house set for a teardown in less than twenty-four hours? How's this supposed to end well? Hmmm…? Okay. Okay, look, James, I'm not a member of your little poetry society here, obviously, but, crass Philistine that I am… I'll give you five thousand dollars to get up, take your backpack, and your sleeping bag, your poetry, and your damned *piss jar*, and quit this house for good. Five thousand dollars. Cash. Under-the-table. I can have it in your hands in an hour. What do you say?

JAMES

Wow.

GINA

Just stay away from here forever. Yes or no?

JAMES

Five thousand—

GINA

Six. Make it six thousand dollars.

JAMES

Wow.

JUNE

Gina, how could we possibly—?

GINA

Not we, Honey. Me. This is strictly my deal. Stay out of it. Whaddya say, James? Six thousand dollars. No tax implications.

JUNE

There's nowhere near that much in the petty cash!

GINA

June! Please! This is not company stuff. I still have a *little* left of my own funds after my loan to you.

JUNE

I—I'm sorry.

GINA

And don't distract me. James: Yes or no?

JOE

(From his prone position on the floor, looking straight up.)

Actually, there would be tax implications.

GINA

Joe, what the hell—?

JOE

There's no "under-the-table" with this guy. I can tell you that. He'd declare it on his taxes. Wouldn't you, James?

JAMES

I declare everything.

GINA

Joe, stay out of this! Please! Yes or no, James?

JAMES

No.

GINA

My god… You're turning down six thousand dollars cash?!

JOE

Sure he is. It's his home.

JAMES

It's my home.

JOE

And it's beautiful. Look at the crown moulding at the ceiling. The door rosettes. Beautiful. Old-school American millwork. Makes me wanna cry. These walls: plaster-on-lath. You can't hire nobody within a hundred miles of here to even do work like that. This floor? Solid oak over southern pine subfloor. And that subfloor's prob'ly two inches thick. A real two-inches. Floor joists are real two-by-eights. They don't mill wood in those dimensions anymore. Those newer additions—the bedroom wing, the new kitchen?—no comparison to the original stuff in here. It killed me to take out those old windows — with the ripple glass? That's antique. Six-over-six. Beautiful. And every muntin in every one of those windows was solid, the glazing tight. You coulda made an aquarium outa those windows and it wouldn'ta leaked. Taking my Sawzall to those porch railings? It was like taking a dentist drill to my own teeth. I don't know if I can do any more…

GINA

What are you saying? You have to take down that last pillar, right?

JOE
(Removes his feet from the coffee table, spins around so he sits side-by-side with JAMES.)

Y'know, I don't think so.

JUNE

Not feeling up to it yet?

JOE

No.

GINA

But later…?

JOE

No, I don't think so.

GINA

Are you serious?! Did you hit yourself in the head along with your damn thumb? What are you saying?

JUNE

I think he's saying he's had an accident today and that he needs a little more time. Right, Joe?

JOE

I'm fine.

JUNE

Good.

JOE

Ultrafine.

JUNE

Okay.

JOE

3M, 800-grit.

JUNE

Okay.

JOE

Wet-or-Dry.

JUNE

Good. Just… okay. Now, James—

(Then, to GINA.)

Gina, are we talking about the cash AND the apartment deal, or—

GINA

The apartment is your deal, the cash is mine. Definitely not both.

JUNE

Right. Now, look, James, so, the apartment offer with the rent-waiver
and caretaking, or the five thousand—

GINA

Six.

JUNE

Six. Six thousand cash. James? Please? How do we resolve this?

GINA

Just listen to Saint June, there, trying to fix everything and everybody.
See, James? Not for nothing did I praise June for her vast superiority
over me in the "Being-A-Person" department. I've never been able to

match her when it comes to things that involve, oh, being a doormat, for example; letting others lead me around by the nose, for example. Sorry, June. That's uncalled for, I know. I don't know how you put up with me. But please, don't be so naïve. Look at him. He's had a thousand chances to come to an agreement with me and he just sits there.

JAMES just sits there, silent.

GINA (cont'd)

Okay, that's it! The shit is now officially hitting the fan… James, I withdraw my offer, and so does June. We must have been out of our fucking minds.

JUNE

No, Gina!

GINA

I'm giving you that five days' notice, James. And that was for you, June, by the way. Me trying to accommodate this criminal? That was me trying to please you. That cash deal was me betraying my every basic impulse. Fool that I am.

JUNE

All right, Gina—

GINA

James: Get the fuck out of my house.

JAMES

It's not—

GINA

NOW! Or I'll tear it down on you myself!

JUNE

Gina, calm down.

GINA

Shut up, June.

JUNE

Gina!

JOE

The Honeymoon is over…

GINA

You think I'm kidding, James? You think I'm not capable of pulling this whole damn house down on you? Right now? MY whole damn house?

JUNE takes hold of GINA's elbow.

JUNE

Gina—

GINA jerks her elbow from JUNE's grip.

GINA

Leave me alone.

JOE

Trouble in Paradise…

GINA

You too, Joe. Get out of my house.

Again, JUNE takes hold of GINA's elbow.

JUNE

Gina.

GINA

What? You going to pull me aside and schoolmarm me again? Do you know how much that annoys me?

JAMES

Please don't fight.

GINA
(To JAMES.)

Another schoolmarm. Shut up, Professor.
(To JOE.)

Now, Joe! Get your crap off the porch and go home. I'm through with you. Your services are no longer required.

JUNE

You don't mean that!

GINA

NOW, Joe!

> *JOE slowly rises from the floor, steadies himself, then walks upstage toward the front door opening. HE stops short of exiting, turns, hesitates.*

GINA (cont'd)

OUT!

> *After another beat, JOE walks right back to where he had been sitting next to JAMES. With resolve, HE resumes his sitting position and folds his arms, in apparent solidarity with JAMES.*

GINA (cont'd)

Holy shit. Seriously?

> *JUNE crosses to JOE's side, crouches beside him:*

JUNE

Joe, just leave for now, okay? Gather your things, put them in your truck and go home. Rest for an hour or two.

JAMES

He shouldn't drive. Those pain-killers he took were actually muscle-relaxants, so...

JUNE

Oh. Oh! See, Gina? He's just a little out of it. I'll drive you home, Joe, okay?

JOE

No. Not going. I'm staying with this guy right here.

> *JOE drapes his arm over JAMES's shoulder.*

GINA

I'll send you a check for work done to date, then we're finished with each other for good. Got it?

JUNE

Just rest up a bit and you can finish this job later. Okay, Joe?

GINA

Don't contradict—! Jeezus, June! You, too: go home.

JUNE

I'm not—

GINA

Go home!

JUNE

Gina! You can't—! Don't you dare talk to me like that!

> *There is a pause. GINA, JAMES, JOE and JUNE seem frozen for a moment… Then:*

GINA

Oops… Sorry, Honey…

> *(GINA waits a bit for JUNE's reply, but none is forthcoming.)*

I said "Sorry…"

JUNE

I heard you…

GINA

You can stay.

JUNE

Of course I can stay!

GINA

Right… I didn't mean to embarrass you.

JUNE

You don't embarrass me. You embarrass your *self*.

JOE
(Simultaneously with JUNE.)

—*self*. Your self…That was in my head and it just came outta me.

Couldn't help it…

There is a pause…

GINA

Well, this is awkward!

There is a pause…

GINA (cont'd)

All right! Mea culpa, mea culpa, mea maxima culpa! Sorry. Sorry, everybody! So, June, you still want to fix this? Be my guest. He's all yours, Honey. I'll just retire to my corner…

GINA crosses to the chair by the window.

GINA (cont'd)

Who knows? I'll just observe… maybe learn how to be a better person… Hmmm…? Who knows…?

SHE sits.

JUNE

How do you feel, Joe?

JOE

Superfine.

JUNE

600-grit, huh?

JOE

3M, wet-or-dry.

JUNE

Can you handle your tools? Is your thumb still a problem?

JOE

No.

JUNE

No, can't handle tools? or, No, thumb's not a problem?

                          JOE

No, thumb's not a problem, you fixed it, thanks, and no, can't tool
my... can't... handle my... tools...

                          JUNE

Mm hmm. What's left to do?

                          JOE

The last temporary is in place but it needs to be clinch-nailed, then
the pillar needs to be removed. And that's the last one.

                          JUNE

How long would that take?

                          JOE

Half-hour. Hour, tops.

                          JUNE

Could you do it, say, two or three hours from now? Or sometime
before dark?

                          JOE

Yeah, I prob'ly could.

                          JUNE

Great.

                          JOE

But I won't.

                          JUNE

What?

                          JOE

My services are no longer offered.

                          GINA

Hah!

                          JUNE

Oh...

GINA

(Mock applauding.)

Well done, Young Lady! Well done, Saint June!

JUNE

Then... you'll have to leave.

JOE

No. I'm with James, here.

JUNE

Oh, Joe, please don't do this.

GINA

Oh, June, please don't do that! Have some balls, already!

JAMES

Joe, you don't have to—

JOE

I'm with you, Pal. You got balls!

JAMES

Thanks...

JOE

Is there any more of that pizza? I'm feeling a little puny. Those pills...

JAMES

Oh, yeah...

(HE hands the box to JOE.)

Help yourself...

JOE

Thanks...

(HE eats.)

GINA

Oh, perfect! This is perfect! Look at them, June, just look at them! A couple of hopeless Losers – sitting on the floor eating greasy pizza.

And y'know what? They actually think they're superior to you and me. They're judging us.

JUNE

I don't think they're judging—

GINA

You, too, Saint June. You've had to stifle yourself for a while now, huh? Been hard to be my partner? Watching me build everything up for us? Had to hold your tongue a lot, huh, Junebug? Didn't want to seem judgmental? Well, I appreciated that and I loved you for it. I hope you know that. Even though I did think it was just the littlest bit mousy of you... See, I was hoping maybe you'd get it after a while — how things actually work. I mean, Jeez you're a slow learner! I'm giving you a lesson now, too, but there you are, judging me. I'm surprised you're not sitting on the floor with these other two, looking down on me, just like them...

> *Keeping her eyes locked on GINA's eyes, JUNE crosses to stage right of JAMES and sits down on the floor next to him, then folds her arms, in defiant solidarity with JAMES and JOE.*

GINA (cont'd)

Okay... Okay... I deserved that...

(A little laugh.)

You always take me so literally, June, for heaven's sake...

> *JUNE reaches for the pizza box, removes a slice and takes a bite...*

GINA (cont'd)

Oh, please, June, don't be so childish...

> *JUNE chews...*

GINA (cont'd)

Okay, I get it: "My Bad." Sorry...

> *GINA stands and crosses to JUNE.*

Now let's go…

GINA takes JUNE's arm and tries to pull her up from the floor.

GINA
JUNE

Get your hand off of me, Gina.

GINA tugs a little harder.

GINA

Come on, Honey.

JUNE

I said GET your hand OFF of me!

GINA let's go, steps back quickly.

GINA

Whoa! Where did that come from? Hey, who are you? Did you usurp my wife's body, or something? Where's my little Junebug?

JUNE

Get away from me, Gina.

GINA moves away a bit.

GINA

Okay! I'm sorry…

There is a silence. JUNE puts the half-eaten slice of pizza back in the box. JAMES tears off a sheet of paper towel and hands it to JUNE, then tears off another one and hands it to JOE. JUNE and JOE use the paper towel sheets to wipe pizza grease from their fingers…

GINA (cont'd)

All right…

(A little laugh.)

Lunch over? Symbolic gestures made? Everybody satisfied? Then let's go, June. You can't stay here all day.

                              JUNE
If James stays, I do, too.

                              JOE
Me, too.

        (HE pumps a fist into the air:)
Solidarity!

        (HE pumps his other fist into the air:)
Occupy!

        (HE pumps both fists into the air:)
Ya-a-a-a-y!

                              JUNE
I don't want to be anywhere near you right now, Gina, and I don't know when I'll feel any differently. Go home. Leave me alone.

                              GINA
Well, you know what, Honey? Technically, I *am* home. This is my house, and you all are not welcome here! So, all of you, get the fuck out of my house!

        JAMES, JOE and JUNE remain sitting.

                         GINA (cont'd)
Dammit, I swear, I will tear this house down myself! I will! I'll bring the roof down on all three of you. Get out of here!

        JAMES, JOE and JUNE remain sitting. Suddenly GINA
        dashes through the doorway and out to the porch. JAMES,
        JUNE and JOE listen as GINA can be heard stomping
        around, muttering and cursing:

                         GINA (cont'd)
                        (From offstage.)
...the three of you!...now, where the fuck?...dammit!

GINA charges back into the living room, shouts at JOE:

GINA (cont'd)

Joe, where is your, your, your — THING?! That, sludge — thingie? Hammer? Sludge—?

JOE

Sledgehammer?

GINA

Where is it?

JOE

On the porch, near that last pillar.

GINA again bolts from the living room out to the porch. JAMES, JOE, JUNE remain sitting, looking toward the doorway where GINA exited. THEY hear GINA stomping around on the porch, then a brief silence, followed by one heavy sledgehammer blow.

GINA
(From offstage.)

I swear, June, I'll tear it down! Get them out!

Hammer blow.

GINA (cont'd)
(From offstage.)

Now! Out, dammit!

Hammer blow.

JAMES

Can she really...?

JOE

Well... the porch roof? Sure, if she knocks out all those temporaries...

JUNE

But they're secure, right?

Hammer blow.

JOE

They're clinch-nailed to the deck and header, but they could be whacked out, I suppose, if someone was really—

Hammer blow.

JOE (cont'd)

—if someone was really trying.

JUNE

I think she's really trying.

Hammer blow. A few wisps of dust fall from the ceiling. (See Production Notes*)

GINA
(From offstage.)

See what you're making me do, June?

Hammer blow. More debris falls from the ceiling.

GINA (cont'd)
(From offstage.)

Get them out of there! NOW!

Hammer blow, followed by more debris falling from the ceiling. JAMES, JOE and JUNE are becoming apprehensive.

GINA (cont'd))
(From offstage.)

Don't make me do this, June!

Hammer blow; small chunks fall from the ceiling. (See Production Notes*)

JAMES

Is the whole house coming down?

JOE

Naw, the ceiling's just cracking a little. This part of the house is strong. The additions, not so much. But if the porch roof goes, pivots down, hits the side of the house? Dominoes… y'know?

Hammer blow; debris falls from the ceiling; a loud CRASH! from the porch; more debris falls.

JOE (cont'd)

Oh, boy. There went a temporary…

Hammer blow; debris.

JOE (cont'd)

If she knocks out a couple more…

Hammer blow; debris.

JUNE

She won't stop. I know her.

GINA
(From offstage.)

I won't stop, Honey — not till you're all out of there…!

Hammer blow; cracking noises; debris falls from the ceiling.

GINA (cont'd)

You and your COMRADES…!

Hammer blow; cracking noises; debris.

JOE

That porch roof weighs a fuckin' ton…

Hammer blow.

JUNE
(*Urgently, to JAMES.*)

I can't stop her, James! I'm begging you — get up, go out there, tell her it's over! *Please*, James!

JAMES

It's *not* over.

Hammer blow.

JUNE

I swear, James, if Gina hurts herself out there, if she so much as breaks a fingernail, I'll—! Get up! *Go!*

Hammer blow; debris.

JAMES

She won't hurt herself. She's not that crazy.

JUNE

Yes, she is!

JOE

Actually, she is.

Hammer blow.

JOE, still woozy, struggles to his feet, heads for the doorway.

JOE

I'll stop her... I'll... grab her...

HE steps out to the porch. JUNE stands up.

JUNE

Don't hurt her, Joe!

Hammer blow; debris.

GINA
(From offstage.)

Stay away from me Joe! Don't you even THINK about it!

JOE backs into the house from the porch.

JOE
Oh, boy. She swings that sledge like she's goin' to the Olympics.

JOE sits heavily back on the sofa.

Hammer blow.

JUNE
(Draws close to JAMES.)

Six months. Rent free. Gina does not speak for me. I have not
withdrawn *my* offer. One unit in *my* apartment building, rent free, six
months. No caretaking. But you have to leave now!

Hammer blow; debris.

JUNE (cont'd)
I'll report it to the IRS as payment to you, and you can declare it as
income with your tax return. All legal. All above board. Okay?

JOE
Take the deal! Don't be such a tightass.

JUNE
Will that work for you?!

Hammer blow; debris; CRACK!

JOE
Jeezus… James, look, I can't— I got a wife and three kids at home…

JAMES
(To JUNE.)

You're sure you can—?

JUNE

YES, I'M SURE! It's my building! Six months free! Will that work for you?!

Hammer blow; more cracking noises.

JOE

This is gettin' kinda bad.

JAMES

...Alright. Alright. Yes. Thank you.

JUNE

Go, then! GO!

JAMES begins to gather things and stuff them into his backpack.

JAMES

(HE shouts to GINA.)

ALL RIGHT! STOP! I'M COMING OUT!

JAMES wriggles out of his sleeping bag.

Hammer blow; cracking noises; debris; CRASH!

JOE

A-a-and another one.

JAMES stands.

JAMES
(To GINA.)

WE'RE COMING OUT!
(To JUNE.)

Thank you. Thank you!

JUNE

Go to the office. Joe — you go with him. I'll have something for you, too. Go! GO! I'll meet you there.

Hammer blow; cracking noises; debris.

GINA
(From offstage.)
I'm making a lot of PROGRESS out here!

JAMES
Joe, let's go.

JAMES grabs JOE by the hand — the wrong one:

JOE
AAAAH!

JAMES
Sorry!

(Shouts to GINA.)
STOP! WE'RE COMING OUT!

Hammer blow, debris.

JAMES (cont'd)
ALL RIGHT! STOP!

JAMES grabs JOE's other hand and helps JOE to his feet.

Hammer blow, debris.

JUNE
GINA! STOP! HE'S DONE!

SHE rushes out through the doorway. JOE staggers a little, then sits on the sofa. HE packs up his first aid kit as HE speaks to JAMES.

JOE
I wanna say, you're doin' the right thing here, takin' that offer. I knew you weren't a total asshole. And she's good people, that June is. Good people.

JAMES hoists his backpack.

JAMES

Get up, Joe. Let's go.

HE grabs JOE by the hand — the wrong one:

JOE

AAAAAH!

JAMES

Sorry! Come on!

HE grabs JOE's other hand and helps JOE to his feet, just as GINA rushes in through the doorway, followed close behind by JUNE. GINA is carrying JOE's sledgehammer. SHE crosses to the fireplace, turns to face JAMES, JOE and JUNE.

GINA

I warned you I'd tear this place down myself! Didn't I? So glad you got the message! Now get out! Get out of my house!

JAMES heads for the door. JOE spots JAMES's sleeping bag on the floor and goes to retrieve it. GINA raises the sledgehammer in threat.

GINA (cont'd)

OUT!

JOE freezes.

JAMES

Leave it, Joe. Let's go.

JOE joins JAMES. THEY exit. GINA and JUNE lock eyes across the room, GINA breathing heavily after her exertion...

GINA

And that's... how you... how you do... *that*...! I knew he'd back down... I knew it! Just stand your... stand your ground and they all give up... sooner or later... "Principle?!" Don't they just crawl up your ass?... People like that? Don't you just... loathe them... just a little...?

(*Laughs.*)

Ha haa! Scared the shit outa that asshole, didn't I?

JUNE

I told him I'd give him a six months free rent deal.

GINA

You *what*?

JUNE

With no caretaking.

GINA

The fuck you did.

JUNE

I told him my offer was still on the table, he accepted.

GINA

...Well, well, well... That fucking hypocrite.

(*A little laugh.*)

You see, Honey? How quickly they drop their precious principles when their world comes crashing down around their heads!? What an insufferable prick. Would hate to "take advantage" of someone else's "misfortune!" God, they all make me sick! But—Wow, Junebug! Wow! You're a quick study after all! My deepest apologies! You got the fucker off his sorry ass and out of the house! Aren't you a sweet little Machiavelli?!

JUNE

I'm going to meet him at the office and make it formal.

GINA

No, you're not.

JUNE

And I'm giving Joe a bonus. Hazard pay. Five hundred dollars. From petty cash.

GINA

Are you out of your fucking *mind*?!

THEY stare at each other, GINA still holding the sledgehammer.

JUNE

…Don't talk to me like that…

GINA

Have you forgotten the terms of the loan I gave you so you could buy that place? The contract?

JUNE

No.

GINA

The clause that states I have the right of refusal concerning tenants?

JUNE

I know. I don't care.

GINA

Oh my god… Look at you. My little little Junebug has flown away! Buzzed off! I should be PROUD of you. In fact, maybe I *am*, a little. But you're not going to do this, Honey. I can forgive you, you got him out of the house. But I will not approve of that bastard as a tenant, so you will make no deal!

JUNE retrieve's JAMES's sleeping bag from the floor, gathers her things from the coffee table.

JUNE

Try and stop me.

Dragging the sleeping bag, JUNE heads for the doorway.

GINA

June! No! JUNE! DON'T WALK OUT ON ME!

JUNE halts.

GINA (cont'd)

Don't go, June! Please! I beg you!

JUNE turns, faces GINA.

GINA (cont'd)

Oh, Honey, I — I think I, I might have, maybe, scared the shit out of you, too. Huh? A little bit?

(JUNE is silent.)

Okay. Sorry.

(A little laugh.)

Scared myself, too… a little bit.

(SHE hefts the sledgehammer, feeling its weight.)

Kinda got into the… the swing of it. But what teamwork, huh? We're so good together! Good cop, bad cop, right…?

(JUNE is silent.)

Mmmmm… So, Good Cop made a little side deal, huh…?

(Silence.)

…You know — that clause in our contract? — that's there for your protection, June. I insisted on it because I don't want you to get hurt. Look, I don't give a fuck about free rent or whatever, but a contract is a contract. We made a deal. You have every right, now, to let that bastard know your hands are tied, legally, and you have to cancel. I leave it up to you. But — and it would *kill* me to do it — but, if you don't honor the terms of our mutual agreement, and you cross me, betray me… I will cancel you, Honey. One phone call from me to the scary lawyers and anything you sign will be dead before the ink is dry. And I will sue you for breach of contract. It's the principle of the thing. But… stop this now?… come home with me?… leave him to stand alone all night at the office door?… all will be forgiven. By tomorrow, all will be forgotten…

THEY are facing each other across the room, GINA still holding the sledgehammer, JUNE holding the sleeping bag. There is a pause, then:

JUNE

How sweet that would be for you, hmm? You: my protector again —
my mentor and my guide; and a decent human being after all, despite
all outward appearances…

> *JUNE, the sleeping bag still in hand, heads for the
> doorway, then stops, turns to GINA:*

JUNE (cont'd)

I'm on my way to work, Gina. I have business to take care of. Papers
to sign. You don't like it? Fucking sue me.

> *SHE heaves the sleeping bag over her shoulder and exits.*

> *GINA, still holding the sledgehammer, stands a moment
> looking after JUNE, then SHE crosses up to the sofa and
> sits heavily, the sledgehammer across her lap.*

GINA

Go… Go… My god, another one… Another Loser… How they
exhaust me…

> *(SHE shouts toward the doorway:)*

I WILL! I'LL SUE YOUR ASS OFF! I'M MAKING THE CALL
RIGHT NOW!

> *(SHE doesn't make the call…)*

All of them. They just drain me. Like I'm trying to pull a goddam
herd of ELEPHANTS out of QUICKSAND and they do absolutely
nothing to HELP ME! Work my ass off… Try to make something
great…

> *(SHE shouts toward the doorway:)*

IT'S A TWO-WAY STREET, YOU KNOW…! MARRIAGE…! Two
way street…

> *(SHE ponders the sledgehammer on her lap.)*

Tear it all down… I will… They want it all for free… What's *wrong*
with these people?!

(Again SHE shouts toward the doorway.)

YOU SIGNED A CONTRACT! DOES THAT MEAN NOTHING TO YOU?!

(SHE goes quiet, ponders the sledgehammer. Then, a little laugh…)

Ha, ha… Good for you, Jooney, June, June. Good for you. You learned something after all. I *am* proud of you…

(Again, SHE shouts toward the doorway:)

I'M MAKING THE CALL RIGHT NOW! YOU WON'T DO THIS TO ME! DAMMIT!

> *GINA stands up at the sofa, and with a mighty heave, throws the sledgehammer across the coffee-table to the floor, where it lands with a loud thump.*

> *Suddenly there is a tremendous CR-R-R-R-A-A-ACK!! emanating from the porch*

GINA (cont'd)

Oh shit…

> *GINA moves tentatively toward the doorway, but a deafening, thunderous NOISE bellows from the porch, and plumes of dust (See Production Notes*) rush into the house through the doorway and window. GINA stops dead in her tracks.*

GINA (cont'd)

FUCK me!

> *All light that once came from the window and doorway is extinguished. The porch roof has collapsed and crashed into the side of the house. GINA's exit is blocked.*

> *SHE turns and heads toward the upstage hallway. There comes a CR-R-A-A-ACK—BOOM! from the hallway. A plume of dust (*) rushes from the hallway. Any light from that hallway is now extinguished.*

*Again GINA turns and heads toward the downstage
kitchen arch. There comes a CR-R-A-A-ACK—BOOM!
from the kitchen. A plume of dust (*) rushes from the
archway into the living room. All light from the kitchen
area is extinguished. Again, GINA is blocked, trapped.*

GINA (cont'd)

No! NO!

*SHE returns to the center of the living room. Debris falls
from the ceiling. The room is dim, fogged with dust (*).
GINA spins helplessly, realizing her situation. Suddenly
there is a CR-R-A-A-ACK! from above, and a piercing
shaft of light penetrates the fog, as though the ceiling and
roof has begun to open up to the daylight.*

GINA (cont'd)

No, no…

*Several more CR-R-A-A-ACK! sounds as more shafts
of daylight, in rapid succession, pierce the fog. A deep,
throbbing, subwoofer rumbling begins and grows louder.*

GINA (cont'd)

No, no, no, NO, *NO-O-O-O!*

*Now the profound rumble reaches a crescendo, as if the
house itself were groaning in pain. A cacophony of CR-R-
A-A-ACKING! fills the room. With each CRACK!, more
shafts of daylight pierce the fog, forming a pattern around
GINA that resembles the bars of a prison cell.*

*GINA stops turning, faces full out, raises high her clenched
fists.*

GINA (cont'd)

I JUST PAID A FORTUNE FOR A WRECKING CREW!

*SHE covers her head with her arms. A shrieking CR-R-
R-A-A-A-A-CK from above. GINA, shielding her head,
screaming, crouches to the floor.*

> GINA (cont'd)

AAAAAAAAAAAAH!

> *In her crouch, GINA continues to scream, while, unnoticed by her, all other sounds cease...*

> *GINA's scream gradually grows quieter.*

> GINA (cont'd)

A-A-A-a-a-a-ah...

> *SHE goes completely quiet. There is a deafening SILENCE for a few beats...*

> *GINA looks cautiously skyward...*

> *Silence...*

> *GINA tentatively uncovers her head...*

> *Silence...*

> *GINA very cautiously stands up, looks up, looks left and right...*

> *Silence...*

> *GINA looks straight out at the audience.*

> *The slightest trace of a smile begins to spread across GINA's face...*

> *A few beats of silence... then—*

> *Blackout.*

END OF PLAY.

*Production Notes:

— If projection equipment is available, the art on the walls, the oriental rug, etcetera, indicated in the "dream sequence" can be as elaborate and detailed as desired. Otherwise, lighting effects alone can establish the atmosphere.

— A simple "snow" device, or several devices in different locations in the grid above the stage, may be rigged to produce "debris" sifting from the ceiling.

—If projection capability is available, visible cracks in the walls may appear.

— Electromagnet "traps" in the grid could be rigged to drop small chunks of "plaster" to strategic, non-actor-occupied, locations on the stage floor.

—"Dust" produced by the offstage collapsing structures should be simulated with simple stage smoke, or stage fog, pumped into the room from the areas indicated in the script. The resulting fog will be the perfect medium to capture the "prison bar" shafts of light.

Acknowledgments

I wish to thank, foremost, my bawdy American poet friend Fred Rosenblum for his support and advocacy for my work, without which the publication of this volume would not have happened. Thank you, Fred.
And thank you, Marc Estrin and Donna Bister of Fomite for your sharp-eyed editorial work which improved every aspect of my originally submitted material.

I gratefully acknowledge, too, Curt Columbus and Tyler Dobrowsky of Trinity Repertory Company for encouraging me as an "emerging" playwright! Your generous gifts of your time and insight have helped me immeasurably.

Furthermore, to the administrative staff and the artists of Trinity Repertory Company who have been my colleagues over the years and who contributed to the success of my play workshops — my deepest thanks.

And integral to the development of the plays in this volume are Esteban Alvarado and the insanely talented writers in Esteban's Writers Workshop at San Diego College of Continuing Education. Thanks, all, for your enthusiastic support!

And ultimately — thanks to Cynthia, whose infallible sense of truth and beauty in art has kept me, mostly, from going too far astray.

About the Author

In a career spanning four decades as a member of the renowned Trinity Repertory Company's resident acting ensemble, William Damkoehler appeared in well over a hundred productions, either in Trinity's home spaces in Providence, RI, or with the company on Broadway, at the Edinburgh Theatre Festival in Scotland, in Boston, in Philadelphia, or on the venerable Straw Hat Summer Theater Circuit. Favorite roles include Ebenezer Scrooge, Macheath, George Antrobus and James Tyrone in *A Christmas Carol, The Threepenny Opera, The Skin Of Our Teeth*, and *Long Day's Journey Into Night*, respectively. At Trinity, William also served as Director or Musical Director for many main-stage productions.

As a Theater Educator, William held for many years the position of Senior Lecturer at Rhode Island School Of Design where he established an ongoing Acting and Theater Production elective program in the Liberal Arts Division. He created and directed a touring group of senior citizens who performed "kitchen band" music and wrote and performed their own short comedies around the state in the Cranston, RI chapter of RSVP, the original federal Retired Senior Volunteer Program. He also taught and directed at Rhode Island College.

In addition to his playwriting, William's free-lance writing saw non-fiction articles published in *The Providence Journal-Bulletin* and *The New York Times*. Excerpts of other fiction appear in the anthologies *For The Love Of Writing* and *The Stories Start Here*.

William currently lives in San Diego, California with his wife, Cynthia Strickland — also retired from Trinity Rep's acting ensemble.

Fomite

Writing a review on social media sites for readers will help the progress of independent publishing. To submit a review, go to the book page on any of the sites and follow the links for reviews. Books from independent presses rely on reader-to-reader communications.

For more information or to order any of our books, visit:
http://www.fomitepress.com/our-books.html

More plays from Fomite...
Stephen Goldberg — *Screwed and Other Plays*
Michele Markarian — *Unborn Children of America*